Irena Sendler

BRINGING LIFE TO CHILDREN OF THE HOLOCAUST

By Susan Brophy Down

Crabtree Publishing Company
www.crabtreebooks.com

Author: Susan Brophy Down
Publishing plan research and development:
  Sean Charlebois, Reagan Miller
  Crabtree Publishing Company
Project coordinator: Mark Sachner, Water Buffalo Books
Contributing writer: Diane Dakers
Editors: Mark Sachner, Lynn Peppas
Proofreader: Rachel Eagen
Indexer: Gini Holland
Editorial director: Kathy Middleton
Photo researcher: Mark Sachner
Designer: Alix Wood
Production coordinator: Margaret Amy Salter
Prepress technician: Margaret Amy Salter
Print coordinator: Katherine Berti

Written, developed, and produced by Water Buffalo Books

A special note of thanks to filmmaker Mary Skinner,
2B Productions, who shared photos and details of Irena
Sendler's story in the spirit of her promise to Mrs.
Sendler—to help young people learn more about the
Holocaust, the anguish of Jewish mothers and their
children, and the noble Poles who fought to save them.

Publisher's note:
All quotations in this book come from original sources and
contain the spelling and grammatical inconsistencies of the
original text. The use of such constructions is for the sake
of preserving the historical and literary accuracy of the
sources.

Cover: By the time of her death at the age of 98 in 2008,
Irena Sendler, shown left in 1943–1944, had been
recognized around the world for her efforts in helping
Polish Jews during World War II. Her most notable
achievement was her role in the rescue of about 2,500
children from the Warsaw Ghetto. In the photo on the
right, one of the best-known and most dramatic to come
out of World War II, a group of Jews, including children,
is shown being rounded up by the Nazis following the
Warsaw Ghetto Uprising in 1943.

Photographs and reproductions:

Courtesy of 2B Productions: page 72; page 74; page 85 (all);
  page 100 (all); page 102 (top)
Courtesy of 2B Productions, from the family collection of
  Janina Zgrzembska: cover (left); page 1; page 5; page 17;
  page 37; page 53; page 57 (right); page 77; page 82 (left);
  page 87 (top); page 88 (top); page 99; page 102 (inset)
Creative Commons (Wikipedia): pages 8
  (left), 9, 13, 21, 22, 23, 32, 33, 35, 39 (bottom), 40 (top),
  42, 47 (top, center left, center right), 43, 51, 66, 57, 70
  (left) 71, 81 (top), 102; Mariusz Kubik: page 11, page 101
  (bottom), page 102 (left); Daniel Ullrich, Three Dots:
  page 34 (top); Kitkatcrazy: page 34 (second from top);
  page 34 (second from bottom); The devious diesel: page
  34 (bottom); page 55 (right); page 59; page 73; page 82
  (right); Deutsche Fotothek☐: page 83; page 84 (upper left
  and lower right); page 97 (both);
Getty Images: page 4
Public domain: front cover (right); page 8 (right); page 12;
  page 14; page 15; page 18; page 20; page 24; page 25;
  page 26; page 29 (all); page 30; page 39 (top); page 40
  (bottom); page 44; page 45; page 46; page 47 (bottom);
  page 49; page 54; page 55 (left); page 56; page 57 (left);
  page 61; page 62; page 63; page 65; page 68; page 69
  (both); page 70 (right); page 75; page 78; page 79; page
  80; page 81 (top); page 84 (upper right); page 87
  (bottom); page 88 (bottom); page 89; page 90; page 91;
  page 93; page 95 (both); page 96

Library and Archives Canada Cataloguing in Publication

Down, Susan Brophy
  Irena Sendler : bringing life to children of the Holocaust / Susan
Brophy Down.

(Crabtree groundbreaker biographies)
Includes index.
Issued also in electronic formats.
ISBN 978-0-7787-2553-4 (bound).--ISBN 978-0-7787-2556-5 (pbk.)

  1. Sendlerowa, Irena, 1910-2008--Juvenile literature. 2. Righteous
Gentiles in the Holocaust--Poland--Biography—Juvenile
literature. 3. World War, 1939-1945--Jews--Rescue--Poland--Juvenile
literature. 4. Holocaust, Jewish (1939-1945)--Poland--Juvenile literature. 5. Jewish
children in the Holocaust--Poland--Warsaw--Juvenile literature. 6. Warsaw
(Poland)--History--Juvenile literature. I. Title. II. Series: Crabtree groundbreaker biographies

D804.66.S46D69 2012   j940.53'18092   C2012-901520-2

Library of Congress Cataloging-in-Publication Data

Down, Susan Brophy.
Irena Sendler : bringing life to children of the Holocaust / Susan
Brophy Down.
  p. cm. -- (Crabtree groundbreaker biographies)
Includes index.
ISBN 978-0-7787-2553-4 (reinforced library binding : alk. paper) --
ISBN 978-0-7787-2556-5 (pbk. : alk. paper) -- ISBN 978-1-4271-7861-9
(electronic pdf) -- ISBN 978-1-4271-7976-0 (electronic html)
1. Sendlerowa, Irena, 1910-2008--Juvenile literature. 2. Righteous
Gentiles in the Holocaust--Poland--Biography--Juvenile literature. 3.
World War, 1939-1945--Jews--Rescue--Poland--Juvenile literature. 4.
Holocaust, Jewish (1939-1945)--Poland--Juvenile literature. 5. Jewish
children in the Holocaust--Poland--Warsaw--Juvenile literature. 6.
Jews--Poland--Warsaw--History--20th century--Juvenile literature. 7.
World War, 1939-1945--Poland--Warsaw--Juvenile literature. 8.
Warsaw (Poland)--History--Juvenile literature. I. Title.

D804.66.S46D69 2012
940.53'18092--dc23
[B]
                                    2012008274

Crabtree Publishing Company

www.crabtreebooks.com   1-800-387-7650   Printed in Canada/042012/KR20120316

**Published in
Canada
Crabtree Publishing**
616 Welland Ave.
St. Catharines, ON
L2M 5V6

**Published in the
United States
Crabtree Publishing**
PMB 59051
350 Fifth Avenue, 59th Floor
New York, New York 10118

**Published in the
United Kingdom
Crabtree Publishing**
Maritime House
Basin Road North, Hove
BN41 1WR

**Published in
Australia
Crabtree Publishing**
3 Charles Street
Coburg North
VIC, 3058

Contents

A collage of photographs of Irena Sendler, along with the cover of a book published about her in Poland, on display at a reception in ____. At the time, Irena was being awarded the Order of the Smile, an international prize presented to adults for the love, care, and help they have given to children. By the time of her death at the age of 98 in 2008, Irena had been recognized around the world for her efforts in helping Polish Jews during World War II. Her most notable achievement was her role in the rescue of about 2,500 children from the Warsaw Ghetto.

MATKA
DZIECI HOLOCAUSTU
Historia Ireny Sendlerowej

Chapter 1
The Toolbox Baby

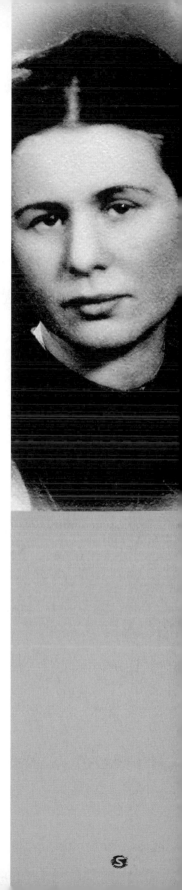

Summer, 1942. To the German soldiers standing guard in Nazi-occupied Warsaw, Poland, the Polish carpenter carrying his tools didn't arouse suspicion at all. The tradesman calmly hoisted his toolbox onto the load of bricks in the back of his truck and drove away. What the soldiers didn't know was that inside the box was not a hammer, saw, and other tools, but a six-month-old baby sleeping soundly, drugged so she wouldn't cry and draw attention. The baby's mother also lovingly placed a silver spoon in the toolbox-crib, a spoon etched with the family's name. She hoped to be reunited with her child after the terrible conflict that was raging in much of the world at that time. That conflict was World War II, and it would claim the lives of tens of millions of civilians by the time it ended in 1945.

Saving the Children

Many dramatic escapes like this were successful because of the work of a devoted group of people led by Irena Sendler. In this case, the baby got out safely, driven away from the walled-in ghetto the Germans had created for the Jewish population of occupied Poland. Her Polish rescuers brought them to the relatively safer Christian area, although this was also under German control.

A Portrait of World War II

On September 1, 1939, Nazi Germany attacked Poland, and, as agreed in the German-Soviet non-aggression pact signed in August 1939, the Soviet Union attacked from the east on September 17. On September 3, although Britain and France declared war on Germany in support of Poland, neither country brought real military aid to the besieged country.

That was the beginning of World War II, which lasted in Europe until Germany surrendered on May 7, 1945. The war in Asia continued until Japan—which sided with Germany—formally surrendered on September 2, 1945. During that time, almost every country in the world became involved in the conflict. If a country sided with Germany, it was part of the so-called "Axis." If a country sided with Britain and France, the two major powers first to declare war on Germany, it was one of the "Allies."

The main Axis nations were Germany, Italy, Japan, Hungary, and Romania. The Allies initially consisted of Britain and France. Over the next few years, most of the world's nations joined the Allies. The largest Allied nations—the Soviet Union, the United States, and China—joined the fight in 1941. A year later, 26 Allied countries formed the United Nations. (After the war, another 25 countries joined the UN.)

In Europe, Nazi Germany was highly successful in its efforts to invade and take over countries in all directions. By 1943, the Nazis

Stop this monster that stops at nothing... PRODUCE to the limit !

This is YOUR War!

This U.S. propaganda poster depicts Germany and Japan savagely attacking the Statue of Liberty. The poster's message is intended to spur U.S. workers to give their all to the war effort.

had increased their territory to include most of continental Europe as we know it today. They made a big mistake, though, when they started moving into the Soviet Union in 1941.

When Germany broke its agreement with the Soviets and started invading Soviet-held areas, the Soviet Union joined the Allies in fighting against Germany. That significantly increased the number of forces opposing the Nazi military.

Meanwhile, in Asia, Japan had invaded Manchuria (now northeast China) in 1931, and China in 1937. After World War II started in Europe, Japan joined the Axis, siding with Germany. To try to prevent Japan from dominating Asia, the United States stopped all trade with Japan. The most significant thing the United States did was stop selling oil to Japan, potentially crippling the Japanese military.

In return, to make sure the United States didn't become the dominant force in the Pacific, Japan bombed Pearl Harbor, Hawaii, on December 7, 1941. Japan also formally declared war on the United States. That led Britain, Canada, and the United States to declare war on Japan. Germany and Italy then declared war on the United States, and the United States declared war on those two nations.

Over the next few years, as the Soviets attacked Germany from the east, other Allied forces (Britain, Canada, and the United States, among others) attacked from the west and south, eventually beating the Germans into surrender. Adolf Hitler committed suicide on April 30, 1945. Germany surrendered a week later, marking the end of World War II in Europe.

At the same time, Japan was battling the Allies over Asian land and Pacific islands. Each side won individual battles—until August 6, 1945. That's the day the U.S. Air Force dropped an atomic bomb on Hiroshima, Japan. Three days later, the United States dropped another atomic bomb on another Japanese city, Nagasaki. More than 120,000 civilians died because of those bombs—either during the bombing or from radiation exposure after the bombing.

Within days of the bombings, Japan agreed to surrender to the Allies, and on September 2, 1945, World War II in the Pacific was officially over.

World War II was the biggest war in history. About 100 million military personnel fought in the war, and 50 to 70 million civilians died, making World War II the deadliest war in history. It was also the only war to use nuclear weapons.

Escape By Any Means Possible

Rescuers carried some children out in potato sacks, and some in coffins. Other children escaped through tunnels and even the sewers. The toolbox baby was one of about 2,500 Jewish children from the Warsaw Ghetto saved by Irena Sendler and her team during World War II.

Without Irena's help, these children would surely have died. More than nearly any other conflict in history, World War II was a war waged against children as well as soldiers.

Jewish children are rounded up to be deported out of the Lodz Ghetto in Poland. The destination for deportation from Lodz was Chelmno, which was also in Poland. Chelmno was a German concentration camp set up by the Nazis for one chief purpose—the mass murder of Jews and others, including Poles, Czechs, Soviet prisoners of war, and Romanies (Gypsies).

The Nazis forced Jewish children and their families to live in ghettos throughout Europe. There, overcrowding led to widespread illness and starvation. There was also the threat of being sent to the concentration camps, where Jews were killed in vast numbers.

In Warsaw, Irena was a social worker whose job was to help people in need. New laws imposed by Nazi Germany made it illegal to help Jews, however, so Irena volunteered with a secret group that helped smuggle the Jewish children out of danger. Not only that, but they also helped whole families by providing money and fake identification papers.

The group was also unusual in that it was run by Christians as well as Jews, and their only aim was to work together to sustain and

Two children begging for food or money on a street in the Warsaw Ghetto. Irena's mission was to rescue children like these from certain death in the ghetto or in the extermination, or death, camps, which existed for the sole purpose of killing.

support persecuted Jews. The activities were very risky, and Irena, a young non-Jewish Polish woman, was eventually arrested, jailed, and tortured for her work on behalf of others. Although the Nazis pressured her to give information on her friends who were also working secretly to help the Jews escape, she kept silent.

Irena's father risked his life for others as part of his medical practice.

A Fighting Spirit

When Irena was young, a relative said she was spoiled. Those early happy days only gave her a strength of character that she would rely on later, however, when she was not so pampered. It is not surprising that Irena was willing to take risks to do what she felt was right.

"If someone is drowning, you have to give them your hand. When the war started, all of Poland was drowning in a sea of blood, and those who were drowning the most were the Jews. And among the Jews, the worst off were the children. So I had to give them my hand."

Irena Sendler

Irena Sendler at her home in Warsaw, Poland, on February 15, 2005. On this day, in celebration of her 95th birthday, Irena greeted several family members and guests, including some of the "children" she had rescued during World War II.

THE HOLOCAUST:
HORROR AND SORROW

By the end of World War II, approximately six million Jews had been killed by Nazi Germany, other Axis nations, and those who cooperated, or collaborated, with them. This organized, government-authorized extermination, or mass murder, of Jews became known as the "Holocaust," a word of Greek origin meaning "sacrifice by fire."

Today we understand the need to respect all ethnic and religious groups. That was not, however, the case in Germany before and during World War II. Under the leadership of Adolf Hitler, the Nazi Party promoted the idea of one group that was superior to all others—a "master race" made up of people of northern European descent. Members of this group, called "Aryans" in Nazi propaganda, were set off against other groups.

The Nazis wanted to eliminate those who were different from what they considered the Aryan ideal. They singled out European Jews as the primary targets of their campaigns of threats, deportation, and slaughter. In addition to the Jews, whom they persecuted on ethnic grounds, the Nazis targeted others as well. These included Poles, Russians, Romanies (Gypsies), Jehovah's Witnesses, homosexuals, people with disabilities, and members of certain political groups, such as communists and socialists.

Before World War II began, the Nazis passed a series of increasingly harsh laws that discriminated against Jews in Germany. For example, Jews were not allowed to work for the government, vote, or marry non-Jewish Germans. The number of

In 1941, German soldiers conducted a massacre of more than 2,700 Jews on a beach in the nation of Latvia. The women and girls shown here, surrounded by the bodies of other victims, were among the approximately 75,000 Jews believed to have been killed during the Nazi occupation of Latvia during the Holocaust.

Jewish women are marched through the streets of Nazi-occupied Budapest, Hungary, in 1944, most likely to one of the city's two ghettos. From there, most would be deported to Auschwitz and other Nazi concentration camps. By the end of the war in 1945, hundreds of thousands of Hungary's Jewish population had been killed.

Jewish students at universities was restricted, and Jewish professionals, such as doctors and lawyers, found it difficult to earn a living. By the mid 1930s, many places posted signs that read "Jews Unwelcome." It wasn't until World War II began in 1939, however, that Hitler made clear his ultimate goal—what later became known as the "Final Solution"—the organized mass murder, or genocide, of Jews in all of Europe.

In the early years of the war, the Nazis forced Jews to move into crowded, unsanitary ghettos in German-occupied Poland and parts of the Soviet Union. The most brutal of these ghettos were walled off or surrounded by barbed wire. There, hundreds of thousands died of disease and starvation. In some ghettos, the occupants organized uprisings against the Nazis. All of them failed, and most of those involved in the uprisings were killed.

By the end of the war, most of the ghettos had been emptied of their residents, whom the Nazis killed outright or sent to death camps, where they were killed within hours of arriving. In the camps, many Jews were herded into massive gas chambers, thousands at a time, tricked into thinking they were going to have showers.

The term "Holocaust" initially referred to the genocide against Jews. In recent years, its use has broadened to refer to other civilians selectively chosen by the Nazis for slaughter. Today, memorial groups and museums offer reminders of this terrible chapter in human history, in hopes that it will never be repeated.

Irena's family had a history of taking action to support what they believed in, even if that meant they were punished for it. The Russians had sent Irena's great grandfather to Siberia as punishment after he joined the January Uprising of 1863 against the Russian Empire, which controlled Poland at the time. Her father risked his life for others as part of his medical practice.

Irena had some of that fighting spirit as well. She was outspoken about prejudice, and her views were not always popular with her co-workers later in life. However, Irena learned from her family to decide for herself what was right and to not always assume that the government knew best. She also discovered that helping other people, even if those people came from different cultures and religions, was what she wanted to do with her life. She knew how difficult and dangerous it was to stand up for the rights of others, but she proceeded when it mattered the most, during World War II and afterward. As a result, many children are alive today because of her bravery.

Irena stayed in Poland after the war and continued to work in the medical teaching field. She was responsible for teaching medical experts the best methods for educating their young students. For decades following World War II, however, Poland was under the strict control of its communist government, which was distrustful of people who, like Irena, had fought for a free and independent Poland.

Yad Vashem, Israel's official memorial to the Jewish victims of the Holocaust, also honors gentile, or non-Jewish, heroes who risked their

own lives to save Jews, with the title "Righteous among the Nations." More than 6,000 Poles have been granted this title, more than citizens of any other country. In the 1960s, in recognition of her deeds, Irena was honored as one of those heroes, but she was unable to travel outside communist Poland at the time to attend the ceremony. It would be many years later that she received her award.

Irena's heroism was introduced to a new generation of North American youth when some Kansas high school students created a history project and a play, called *Life in a Jar*, based on her wartime activities. That one project developed into a charity, the Irena Sendler *Life in a Jar* Foundation. This organization continues to reward outstanding teachers and inspire both educators and students to pass on the lessons of respect and understanding of all cultures. Many people around the world have seen the play. There are now several books and a movie about Irena. Her contribution to humanity earned her recognition and awards worldwide.

Chapter 2
Growing Up in Poland

The brave woman who later risked her life for others was born Irena Krzyzanowski near Warsaw on February 15, 1910. Her family was made up of a number of social reformers and activists—people who worked to bring about changes that would improve the lives of others. Irena spent her early years during a period of great political turmoil. At the time, the country of Poland did not exist. The former Kingdom of Poland had been divided up between Russia, Prussia, and Austria for almost 200 years. Poles were not permitted to speak Polish in public, govern themselves, or study their culture. People like Irena's parents preserved their values by forming underground schools, issuing secret publications, and using code words to communicate. Poles would regain their freedom in 1918, only to lose it again when Germany invaded their homeland in 1939.

Family Values

Doing the right thing sometimes made life more difficult in a society where people were expected to think a certain way. Irena's father, Stanislaw, a doctor, understood this well, as his political views had caused him trouble before he finished medical school. His activism on behalf of the poor and less fortunate and his support of Polish independence placed him in conflict with the authorities. As a result, officials didn't allow him to finish his medical training at the university in Warsaw, so he had to travel to another city to complete his degree.

Stanislaw found his ideal mate when he met Janina Grzybowska. Both were members of the Polish Socialist Party (PPS). Janina had worked for an illegal group that continued teaching Polish history and literature when Poland was under the rule of the Russian Empire. They married in 1908. Irena, their only child, was born two years later.

Stanislaw set up a medical practice in a small town near Warsaw. Many of his patients were very poor people who often could not afford to pay him for his services. As a result, his own family was not prosperous, either. In fact, Irena's mother had to sell her own winter coat one year so she could afford to buy enough food for her family. Finally, family relatives offered to buy a large building to house Stanislaw's patients. He turned the building into a hospital to treat people who had lung diseases such as tuberculosis.

The logo of the Polish Socialist Party. Both of Irena's parents belonged to the PPS in the early 1900s. In the 1940s, Irena was also active with the PPS, when it was part of the Polish resistance to the Nazi occupation of Poland.

> *"My father died when I was seven, but I'll always remember him saying that people are divided into good and bad. Nationality, religion or race mean nothing: what kind of person you are is all that counts."*
>
> Irena Sendler

After World War I began in 1914, living conditions worsened for many Polish people. Because Polish territory was partitioned, or divided, between Russia, Prussia, and Austria, much of the heaviest fighting on the war's eastern front lines took place in Poland. As the Russian army retreated, they looted and destroyed many homes under what is known as a "scorched earth" policy. Not only was civilian life in turmoil as the war raged, but food was scarce and a typhus epidemic broke out.

Deadly Epidemics

Although wars cause many deaths on the battlefield, diseases such as typhus are as deadly as gunfire. When people live in dirty and crowded conditions, they are at risk of catching diseases carried by pests such as lice. From the 1500s to the 1800s, epidemics of typhus broke out in Europe, where it was often known as "jail fever." In the early 1800s, during the Napoleonic Wars, more French soldiers died from typhus than from bullets fired by the Russian enemy.

During World War I, typhus killed about three million people in Russia alone. Poland and Romania also experienced deadly outbreaks. Irena's father was one of the only doctors in town willing to make house calls to treat people suffering from typhus. By doing so, he put his own life in danger. He caught the disease himself and died in 1917.

Irena would later help typhus victims herself during her years as an aid worker in World War II. Typhus was common in prisoner of war camps and in the Warsaw Ghetto, where huge influxes of occupants created overcrowding and the unsanitary conditions that spawned the disease. (Scientists discovered an effective vaccine against typhus during World War II, and the disease can now be treated with modern medicine. Even so, typhus still causes about 200,000 deaths each year around the world.)

After Stanislaw's death, Irena's mother continued running the hospital until 1920. She was honored that the Jewish community offered to pay for Irena's education as a way of saying thanks for the treatment Stanislaw provided.

The next year, in 1918, another disease killed millions of people around the world. Much stronger than most of today's colds or flu viruses that might keep people in bed for a few days, the Spanish Flu was fatal for more than 20 million people. In fact, more people died of the flu than were killed in combat in World War I. Irena caught the Spanish Flu and was so ill that doctors cut a hole in her skull (a procedure called trepanning) to ease the effects.

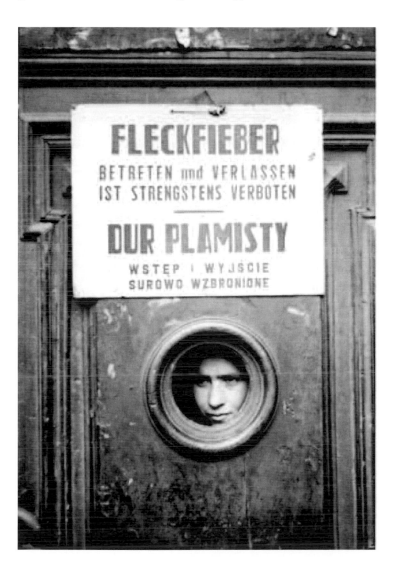

This photo, taken in May 1941, shows a boy peering out from behind a door in the Warsaw Ghetto, where typhus and other contagious diseases were a constant threat. The sign on the door reads, in German and Polish: "TYPHUS. Entering and leaving are strictly forbidden."

This left her with terrible migraine headaches that were so painful she couldn't go to school, so private tutors taught her at home. Still, she was lucky to survive, and her health gradually improved. Although she was plagued with headaches all her life, they were not as intense as when she was a child.

Life in the Face of Tumult

Conflict and political upheaval continued to affect young Irena's life. Her grandfather, Ksawery Grzybowski, moved the family to a new town, taking the last train out of an area that a day later was overrun by Russian fighters during the Polish-Bolshevik War (also known as the War of 1920). Her mother's brother, Irena's Uncle Ksawery, after returning from fighting with Polish forces, also helped make sure that she and her mother had everything they needed. It was only then that Irena attended a real middle school with other children. She remembers this as a very happy time in her life, despite the social turmoil in the country.

Like many children, she loved the scout movement (the Girl Guides and Girl Scouts of today) and its camping and other outdoor activities and group projects. Irena also had a very strong interest in politics. This sometimes got her into trouble, especially when her views were not the same as those of her teachers. When Irena was still in high school, she bought a newspaper and organized a meeting to talk about the May 1926 uprising against the government led by Marshal Jozef Pilsudski, considered by many a hero because of his

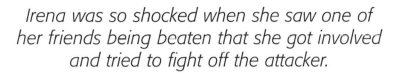

Irena was so shocked when she saw one of her friends being beaten that she got involved and tried to fight off the attacker.

important role in Poland's independence in 1918. Freedom of speech hasn't always been acceptable for students, however, and Irena's headmistress at school suspended her for several days because of her actions.

In 1927, Irena passed her final high school exams. She decided to study law, but after two years at the University of Warsaw, she changed her mind and transferred to the Humanities Department, where she studied teaching and social work.

Life Lessons at the University

Escaping persecution in other parts of Europe, Jews had first come to Poland in the 10th century. There, they enjoyed human rights denied them in other parts of the world. By the 1930s, they made up about 10 percent of Poland's population. In Warsaw, one in every three citizens was Jewish. Most Jews in Poland were Orthodox. They lived in tight-knit communities, speaking their own language, Yiddish, and living according to their ancient customs and traditions.

About 15 percent of Jews in Poland at the time were "assimilated." In other words, they had adopted a modern way of life and attire, spoke Polish, and lived and worked closely with Poles. They were among the country's best-known writers, musicians, actors, directors, and scholars.

Despite the generally favorable climate in Poland for Jews, the 1930s also saw a rise in anti-Semitic incidents in universities and other places where Jews otherwise felt welcome. The Polish government declared at least one group that stirred up harsh feelings against Jews, the National Radical Camp, illegal. Irena was so shocked when she saw one of her university friends being beaten that she got involved and tried to fight off the attacker.

A group of young Jews in the Polish city of Grodno in the 1930s, when it was a center of Jewish life and culture. At that time, about 37 percent of Grodno's population was Jewish. In the course of World War II, when Germany occupied the city, most of its remaining Jewish residents were killed in Nazi concentration camps.

ANTI-SEMITISM: SETTING A PEOPLE APART

Today, the term "Semite" is primarily used to refer to Jews, and an anti-Semite is someone who is prejudiced against Jews. Historically, however, the term "Semite" refers to people connected through languages called Semitic languages. These people include groups living in present-day Ethiopia, Yemen, Oman, Jordan, and Israel, among other places. Semitic languages include Hebrew, Arabic, and Aramaic.

Sadly, anti-Semitism, based mostly on religion, is not a recent phenomenon. Some say it actually started in biblical times. We do know that about 2,000 years ago, in the Roman Empire, conflict erupted when Jews refused to worship Roman gods. Over time, Christianity became the official religion of the Roman Empire, and Rome became the seat of the Catholic Church. For centuries to come, Christians held to the Church's teaching that the Jews were collectively responsible for the killing of Jesus. By government order and due to various forms of persecution, Jews in many Christian countries were forced to flee to other parts of the world.

Since the Middle Ages, campaigns designed to get rid of Jews have occurred time and time again. Thousands of Jews have been killed during these times. Based mostly on religious hatred, anti-Semitism took on yet another form in Europe of the 1800s—prejudice on ethnic or racial grounds. The view of Jews as racially inferior to a mainstream race of white "Europeans" peaked in the most recent mass killing of Jews, during World War II, when Nazi Germany killed six million Jews in the Holocaust.

An anti-Semitic cartoon published in a Nazi newspaper in 1929. The cartoon uses racist imagery to depict two Jewish merchants gloating over the brisk sale of Christmas gifts to non-Jews. It also urges Germans not to do business with Jews.

A student identification card, issued at the University of Warsaw in the 1930s to a Jewish student. The stamp in the upper-left corner indicates that Jewish students were to be seated in a section apart from others. This practice of official segregation, or separation, was called the "ghetto bench" system. It often led to violence directed at Jews. Ghetto benches inspired Irena Sendler, other non-Jewish students, and some professors to voice their opposition to the practice.

Signs of Things to Come In Germany

In Germany, restrictions on Jews had been tightening since Adolf Hitler came to power in the mid 1930s. Attacks on Jewish students and general anti-Semitic behavior had been rampant among civilians as well as soldiers even before the war broke out. Violent riots against Jews, called pogroms, reached a peak in November 1938 when German and Austrian Nazis burned synagogues and Jewish-owned shops. They also ransacked Jewish homes and beat, humiliated, and even killed Jewish citizens, many of them neighbors of those who were tormenting them.

This even happened over two days on November 9 and 10, 1938, and less than a year before World War II broke out. It was thought to be provoked by the assassination in Paris of a German diplomat by a young Polish Jew. The Nazi government did not officially order the pogrom, but it also issued clear instructions to police and military only to interfere if the destruction was directed against non-Jews.

The destruction was known as *Kristallnacht*, or the "Night of Broken Glass." During that pogrom, Nazis killed close to 100 Jews and sent about 30,000 more Jewish men to Dachau and other concentration camps. The Nazis released most of them within several months under the condition that they leave Germany, but not before an estimated total of nearly 2,500 Jews had died as a consequence of Kristallnacht. The rampage also caused the destruction of thousands of Jewish-owned shops and over 200 synagogues in Germany alone.

Irena was so appalled by the events she witnessed on the university campus that she decided to make her own statement in support of Jews.

Time for Others

Irena was so appalled by the events she witnessed on the university campus that she decided to make her own statement in support of Jews. The so-called credit books listing students' grades were clearly marked either

"Once a female Jewish student friend of mine was beaten so severely that I attacked one of the assailants with my fists and spat at his feet, exclaiming, 'You bandit!'"

Irena Sendler

"Jew" or "Aryan" to indicate their ethnic background, and Irena crossed out the word "Aryan" on her book. As a result of her actions, university officials suspended her and refused to allow her to graduate for three years. Finally, in 1939, after she appealed to a new official, she was able to complete her master's degree.

While her studies and her work centered on other people, Irena found time for romance as well. In 1931, she married Mieczyslaw Sendler, a junior assistant at the university whom she had known since childhood. Unfortunately, after a time, they realized their dreams and goals were different, and they lived separately. Irena stayed with her ailing mother in Warsaw, and he joined the army. When Poland's government was forced out of the

Three scenes from the aftermath of Kristallnacht, *the massive anti-Semitic pogrom carried out in 1938 by the Nazis in Germany and Austria.*

Left: *a burning synagogue.*

Below: *a group of Jewish men forced to march on the street carrying a large Star of David.*

Bottom: *men lined up for roll call following their arrest and deportation to the Buchenwald concentration camp.*

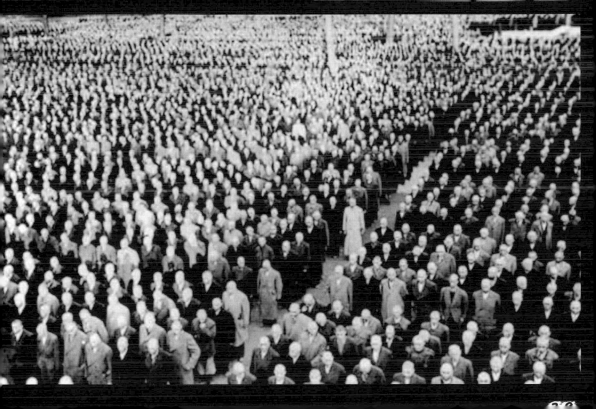

ADOLF HITLER: THE FACE OF EVIL

So terrible were Adolf Hitler's political and racial views, his brutal military tactics, and his crimes against humanity that to many, he represents evil in its purest form. To this day, even his name— Adolf—so strongly brings to mind images of the Holocaust and World War II in general that it is rarely given to newborn babies.

Hitler was born in Austria, in a town near the German border, in 1899. After fighting in World War I, he joined the National Socialist German Workers Party, or the Nazi Party, for short. He worked his way up through the ranks and became party leader.

During his rise to power, Hitler spent time in prison for trying to overthrow the ruling party of Germany. Still, by 1933, the Nazis had enough influence that Hitler became Chancellor, or head of the German government. Following his rise to power, Hitler made it illegal for any political party, other than the Nazi Party, to exist; and so, the "Nazification" of Germany began.

Hitler and his party controlled the content of all newspapers, radio broadcasts, films, art, and books. They broke up trade unions and youth groups, replacing them with single, Hitler-approved organizations. They prohibited churches from preaching anything but Nazi beliefs. Hitler also had the final say in Germany's legal matters, so nobody who opposed him ever received a fair trial. In 1935, laws were passed stripping all Jews of their rights as German citizens and banning them from public transportation and from such public places as theaters, restaurants, and parks.

By the late 1930s, Hitler had begun to ignore international agreements set in place after World War I. In 1938, he took over Austria. A year later, when he invaded Poland, World War II began.

Hitler's attempt to control Europe and rid the world of minorities he considered "inferior" continued for the next five years. Under his orders, millions of Jews were killed. By early 1945, it was clear that the Allies were about to defeat Hitler, Nazi Germany, and the other Axis nations. When Hitler realized he was going to lose the war, he married his longtime companion, Eva Braun. The next day, he shot himself. Eva Braun also killed herself by biting into a cyanide capsule. Days later, Germany surrendered, and World War II ended in Europe.

Adolf Hitler in Paris in 1940, near the start of the German occupation of France.

country and became a government-in-exile following Germany's invasion of Poland in 1939, Mieczyslaw left for the front lines. Within days of the invasion and the start of World War II, Mieczyslaw was captured by the Nazis. He spent four years in a POW (prisoner of war) camp.

Irena had training in education as well as social work, and she looked for a job as a teacher. According to the university, however, her activities as a student fighting prejudice had branded her unacceptable as a teacher due to her political beliefs. As a result, she went into social work instead, and in 1932, she began working for the Mother and Child Aid Society, which was part of the Citizens' Committee for Social Help. This agency assisted the unemployed, providing legal aid to people who had been evicted from their homes. It also offered health care to single mothers and other needy people. The agency acted as a training opportunity for new social work graduates, and Irena thrived in her first

"From the very first day in this job, I was delighted by the wonderful atmosphere of kindness, tolerance, and love for every individual and the spreading of the ideals of goodness and social justice to the entire world."

Irena Sendler

professional job. Her task was to interview people who needed food, shelter, money, and clothing. Later, she was head of the section for unwed mothers.

Irena's employer was full of dedicated employees who did good work, but the politicians of the day were against some of the socialist political views of the staff, and the agency was closed in 1935.

Soon after the agency closed down, Irena began working for the Social Welfare Department for the city of Warsaw. Not only was she a caring social worker, but she also had a broad network of contacts who could help supply food, transportation, and forged, or fake, documents. As conditions worsened for the Jews, Irena's clever schemes and experience grew. These abilities would prove exceptionally valuable in the coming war.

Kindertransport to Safety

With violent anti-Semitic episodes increasing in Germany and other parts of Europe and living conditions becoming worse for many Jewish

> "I was quite absorbed. It was as if I had found myself in another world—a world that was so close to my heart, because it was the one in which I had been raised by my parents."
>
> Irena Sendler

families before the war, parents were already making the decision to send their children away to safety, especially while travel between countries was still possible. One example of a successful escape campaign was *Kindertransport*. This was the informal name for an organization that was unique in that it was run by Jews, Quakers, and Christians. After the series of attacks against Jews known as *Kristallnacht* in November 1938, Jewish groups urged the British government to change the refugee rules to allow Jewish children under the age of 17 into the country. British politicians agreed to the idea as long as homes could be found for them.

British residents responded to the requests and opened their homes to the children. There was no time to waste, and rescues started almost immediately. Transports began less than a month later in December 1938, and they ended when the war began in September 1939. The first transport brought almost 200 children from an orphanage that had been set on fire by the Nazis. Jewish children were transported from Germany, Austria, Poland, and Czechoslovakia (now the nations of Slovakia and the Czech Republic). The group managed to rescue 10,000 children in that short period.

In Poland following the Nazi invasion in 1939, the stakes and risks for Jews and those Poles attempting to help them were higher than ever. Soon the strength and talents of Irena and her co-workers would be put to the greatest test of all.

THE STAR: DISCRIMINATION ON A GRAND SCALE

For centuries, the six-pointed Star of David, named after King David, the biblical Jewish leader, has been a symbol of Judaism and the Jewish people. Long before becoming the commonly known emblem of Jews worldwide that it is today, the star was used in many parts of the Middle East, North Africa, and Europe. It was often used by Jews themselves and frequently as a means of forcing Jews to identify themselves in non-Jewish cultures.

During World War II, all Jews in Germany and most Nazi-occupied territory were forced to sew onto their clothing a yellow badge resembling the Star of David. In Poland, the Nazis forced Jews to wear armbands bearing a blue star. Used this way, the star was a public symbol designed to identify, humiliate, and segregate, or separate, the men, women, and children who wore it. Any Jew who did not display the star could be severely punished—even killed.

The star rule was, at first, only for Polish Jews. In September 1941, Nazi leaders required that it be worn by all Jews in German-occupied territory—anyone over the age of six.

Since the Holocaust, the Star of David has become a symbol of the unity of the Jewish people that is recognized by Jews and non-Jews alike. It is displayed in various forms of ornamentation, including jewelry, and a blue Star of David is part of the flag of the modern Jewish state of Israel.

From top to bottom, Star-of-David badges that the Nazis forced Jews to sew onto their clothing in Germany, France, the Netherlands, and Bulgaria. On the top three badges, the lettering is styled to resemble letters in the Hebrew alphabet.

These children are among the first group of Jews to be rescued by the Kindertransport *program in 1938. They are shown here, exhausted from their trip to England from Germany. Many in this group came from an orphanage in Berlin that had been set on fire by the Nazis. Once in England, they were placed with families, provided an education, and taught trades. Most of them were eventually resettled in Britain and other Western countries, including Canada and the United States. Some of the older children served with the British military in World War II. Their language skills helped Britain in the war effort against Nazi Germany.*

Chapter 3
Early Resistance
1939–1942

Polish territory had been a major battle-ground in World War I, and the scene was about to be replayed in the second major conflict of the century. On September 1, 1939, only a week after Germany and the Soviet Union signed a secret agreement with plans to divide up new territories between them, Germany invaded Poland from the west. This triggered the start of World War II. Two weeks later, the Soviet Union invaded and occupied the eastern part of Poland.

> *"From the autumn of 1939, every act of sympathy toward the persecuted Jews was punishable by death. For handing a Jew a glass of water or a piece of bread you could be killed."*
>
> Irena Sendler

Welfare for the Needy

Irena and her mother heard the frightening news on the radio, and Irena headed for work at the city's Social Welfare Department. She and other staff members had to organize special social welfare points to assist refugees fleeing from other regions of Poland. She would no sooner set up a station than it would be bombed and she would have to find another location. She and her co-workers were also instructed to organize payment to soldiers' wives and families. The president declared that the city administration would remain open day and night. Irena was inspired by his radio broadcasts during the fighting until finally the Nazis bombed the power station and the radio was quiet.

"For the world to be a better place it is essential to love all people and be tolerant."

Irena Sendler

Poland declared war on Germany, and Polish leaders set up a government-in-exile in Britain. From there, they directed a war fought by thousands of Polish soldiers based in other Allied nations, as well as by Polish Home Army resistance fighters in Poland. Polish resistance fighters and civilians alike struggled against the harsh new laws and brutality of the Nazi occupying forces.

Members of the Polish Home Army, the main resistance group against the Nazis in Poland, pose for a photo during World War II. The woman seated with them is a resistance member who risked her own life delivering messages and goods under the noses of German troops.

German soldiers parade through Warsaw during the invasion of Poland in 1939.

German soldiers destroy a barrier, and along with it the Polish coat of arms, at the German-Polish border.

Two Polish soldiers captured during the German invasion in September 1939. In this photo, the two POWs face the German colonel who has just ordered that they be executed.

Almost immediately, Irena volunteered to help the Polish Socialist Party, making deliveries of money or medicine to people in hiding or to families of those who had been killed in the fighting. Her job with the city of Warsaw took on new urgency as well. The city had to fire all its Jewish employees and could not deliver aid to Jewish families. Cutting them off of welfare benefits at a time when they were increasingly unable to care for themselves caused great hardship. In addition to her regular job of making arrangements to care for Polish homeless children, Irena's unofficial job was to help the homeless Jews as well.

At the time, there were only about 20 social aid centers in Warsaw, and these were quickly overwhelmed by needy people. Irena encouraged families in a neighborhood to give what food or medicine they had to each other by matching wealthier families with poorer ones. Her group also had to find food for the Polish POWs whom the Germans had placed in a nearby hospital.

All the volunteer work had to be done with great secrecy, because it was difficult to know who to trust. There were informants everywhere, people who were willing to report to the authorities on their neighbors' suspicious

> *"We were not acting in the name of any political organization but as vocational social workers guided by a sheer sense of humanity."*
>
> Irena Sendler

activities. The Nazis also set up a Jewish police system inside the Warsaw Ghetto, which was built in 1940, forcing the officers to oversee deportations to death camps and other brutal events within the ghetto.

The Tightening Noose

Poland had a very large Jewish population at the time of the Nazi invasion. Jews had made a great contribution to the Polish economy and to Polish culture in general. From the start, the Nazis began a campaign designed to isolate Polish Jews and their way of life. The Germans issued cruel decrees that were printed in a special newspaper.

Each day the rules grew more oppressive. Jewish bank accounts were frozen; no social welfare benefits were available to Jews; Jews were put to work on hard-labor teams; and restrictions on entry and exit cut off the Jewish district from the rest of the city.

Non-Jewish Poles also suffered terribly under the Nazi occupation. Germany's invasion in September 1939 brought bombings and death, much of it in the form of executions, to thousands of Polish citizens. Officials made all citizens abide by a curfew and stay indoors from dusk to dawn. By 1940, the Germans were building new concentration camps not just for Jews but for other Poles as well. The Germans also insisted on a census, or official counting, of the Jewish inhabitants of Warsaw. After that, Jews were issued special identification.

In December 1939, the decrees continued, squeezing the Jews even harder. They couldn't enter post offices, prayer in the synagogues was banned, and all Jewish schools were closed. Lawyers and tailors were not allowed to practice their work. Warsaw Jews were required to wear blue and white armbands with Star of David insignia, signs were required to identify Jewish-owned shops, and train travel was banned.

To get the Jewish people the help they needed, even though they were not allowed any

Two German police officers check the papers of a Jewish Polish woman. Following the German invasion of Poland, the Nazis required Jews to carry official identification and wear a Star of David, like the one on this woman's armband.

social benefits, Irena and her group forged fake ID cards and birth certificates. These documents bore the names of non-Jewish Poles who had recently died. That way, Jews would be eligible for ration cards and other benefits.

In addition to secretly helping Jews, Irena's social work job gave her the opportunity to help others as well. During the early days of the war, homeless refugees inundated Warsaw. Most of them were non-Jews from other parts of Poland who had been bombed out or otherwise displaced by the fighting. Irena's boss had given her added responsibility for these unfortunate people, and she relied on her network of trusted service workers to find them homes and other necessities. She also helped set up a work co-operative to do woodworking and tailoring as a way to keep the young people at home. The Germans wanted to deport them to work elsewhere, but Irena got phony medical certificates made for some to state that they were ill.

Getting into the Ghetto

By November 1940, Jews had been ordered to move their belongings and leave their homes to move into the small section of the city that had become the Warsaw Ghetto. Bricklayers worked to complete a high brick wall topped with barbed wire to completely enclose the area. An estimated 400,000 people were crammed into this space, so that, on average, about eight people had to live in each room.

The ghetto residents' situation was dire. They had no way to earn a living and were not permitted to have social welfare benefits

anymore. It wasn't long before people were starving, and begging children were a common sight in the streets.

Irena managed to get inside the ghetto under the pretext that she was working on public health and fighting diseases. She wore a white nurse's uniform and also put on a yellow armband so she wouldn't stand out among the Jews. The Germans did not want to deal with the dreaded illnesses, such as spotted typhus, that were epidemic in the crowded conditions. By using her credentials as a social welfare worker for the city, Irena was able to smuggle items into the ghetto. She often wore several layers of clothing to give to people inside the ghetto, and the extra padding wasn't detected by watchful guards on her small and slender frame.

Getting Out of the Ghetto

While Irena's efforts to find food and supplies for Jewish families was important work, her greatest achievement was sneaking children out of the Warsaw Ghetto to safe foster homes where they had a chance for survival. There were many children—Jewish and non-Jewish— begging on the streets both inside and outside the ghetto. Everyone was hungry, and many of the children were orphans whose parents had died of disease or been removed to be killed.

THE WARSAW GHETTO

The term "ghetto" refers to an area in a city where people often live in poor conditions. Today, we associate the term with urban areas that are usually inhabited by members of specific racial or ethnic groups. Historically, however, ghettos had their start in European cities where Jews were forced to live. Many areas of Europe, North Africa, and the Middle East had so-called Jewish Quarters where Jews lived following their exile from ancient Palestine (now Israel and parts of other Middle Eastern nations).

The first European Jewish region that was actually called a "ghetto" was in Venice, Italy, in the early 1500s. There, Jews were forcefully segregated, or set apart, mostly on the basis of their being "different" from Venetian society. They lived in poor conditions They were made to wear identifying emblems and submit to laws restricting the kinds of work they could do as well as their movements in and out of the ghetto. At night, Christian officials sealed the ghetto and patrolled the waterways surrounding it to be sure no one entered or left.

During World War II, the Nazis set up ghettos and ordered that Jews live in them. The Warsaw Ghetto was the largest of an estimated 1,000 or more ghettos set up by the Nazis throughout the lands they occupied or controlled.

The Warsaw Ghetto, set up by the Nazis in the fall of 1940, held more than 400,000 Jews. At the time, this was about one-third of the city's population. The Nazis divided Warsaw into three zones—the Jewish, German, and Polish zones. People living outside the ghetto had to carry papers showing they were not Jewish. In Poland, Catholic priests and nuns helped forge thousands of fake documents to aid the Jews. The Nazis eventually built a wall around the Jewish zone, or ghetto, and topped it with barbed wire. Guards manned the entry points, but people escaped through adjoining buildings or sewers.

In January 1943, Jewish resistance fighters within the Warsaw Ghetto launched a revolt against the Nazis. The rebellion lasted several months, but it ultimately failed, and by May it was all over. The ghetto was destroyed, 13,000 Jews died in the uprising, and the survivors were deported to death camps.

Right: Despite hardships of every kind and the ever-present threat of deportation to death camps, residents of the Warsaw Ghetto managed to find ways of entertaining themselves and enriching their lives. Residents formed theater companies and musical events that featured everything from traditional Jewish music to American jazz and cabaret-style music-and-comedy routines like the one shown here.

Above: A young boy holds the head of a teenager who lies ill on a busy street in the Warsaw Ghetto. Many ghetto residents became sick and died from disease and starvation.

Above: Children working as street vendors sold their wares to the only customers allowed to do business with them—other residents of the Warsaw Ghetto.

Above: Captured Jews being herded out of the Warsaw Ghetto by German soldiers during the Nazis' burning of the ghetto in 1943.

To get past the guards and officials, Irena and her group devised different ways to smuggle children out of the ghetto. Rescuers placed the children in a large box or a sack and loaded them on a truck that had brought cleaning supplies. The children were very frightened at being separated from their parents, and if they screamed or cried out, they risked alerting the guards. That's when her truck driver decided to bring a dog with him that would yelp as he drove past the guards so that the children's noises weren't heard. Another favorite plan was to hide a child underneath a stretcher when a sick person was carried away. They were even known to put small babies on the morgue wagons (carts for picking up dead bodies) to sneak them out.

Smuggling children required a vast network of volunteers to act as guides or house the infants once they were free. They brought children to the steetcar station when a friendly driver was on duty. He would sit the child in an empty car and then stop at an isolated spot once outside the ghetto. One of Irena's co-workers, or "co-conspirators," as they called themselves, would be waiting to take the child to a safe home.

Many of the buildings at the edge of the ghetto were next to houses owned by Polish people on the other side, and sometimes it was possible to escape through a basement that connected them. The law courts also had entrances on both the ghetto side and the outside. Court employees who were willing to help these resistance workers and smugglers would guide the ghetto children through the building and out the other side, where another courier would take them to a hiding place.

A remaining section of the wall of the Warsaw Ghetto as it appears today. Like other parts of the wall, this section ran through the backyard of a home. Often Irena and her fellow resistance workers used property shared by both sides of the wall as a means of smuggling children to safety.

Of course, those techniques were suitable only for the smallest children. For teenagers, Irena and her group had to use other methods to help them escape. When they were sent outside the ghetto on work parties, some of the children would not return. As security grew tighter around the ghetto exits, children and their guides would escape through the sewers and emerge through a manhole on the other side.

Many times, aid workers would be waiting to assist them as they came to the surface. To disguise the activities, sometimes a truck would be parked over the hole leading to the sewer.

Inside the ghetto, people's spirits were low. To help the residents help each other, house committees were set up very early in the war. The groups were originally intended to fight fires, build air raid shelters, and perform other defensive tasks. After a while, they functioned as general support groups for an increasingly desperate population. As Irena said, "For hundreds of thousands of people, they served as a refuge where people genuinely helped each other." The house committees also had youth circles that inspired young people to have some hope and enjoy some human dignity. Said Irena:

"In the starving, dying Warsaw
Ghetto these youth circles gave its young
inhabitants the most valuable things
possible: a smile, a sense of joy, and a faith
in humanity."

The Camps: Designed for Terror and Death

Nazi concentration camps were a brutal way to warehouse prisoners and stage murders on a massive scale. Most of the victims were civilians, but they also included POWs. Some camps simply served as venues to hold prisoners awaiting transportation to other facilities. Others were places where victims had to perform hard labor, and some—the most sinister—were extermination, or death, camps, designed for mass murder. When Jews were deported from the Warsaw Ghetto to Treblinka, only those assigned to dispose of bodies lived more than an hour or two after their arrival.

Along with ghettos and planned patterns of persecution, assaults, and killings carried out by Germany during World War II, the concentration camps were key cogs in a systematic program of terror.

Toward the end of World War II, Jews were, by far, the people most often taken to, and killed at, Nazi concentration camps. But the Nazis also targeted political enemies, including communists, socialists, and members of trade unions; POWs (captured Soviet troops were especially singled out for cruel treatment); other groups the Nazis considered inferior "races," such as Poles and Romanies (Gypsies); and other people they felt would dilute the "purity" of the so-called Aryan race—disabled adults and children, homosexuals, and Jehovah's Witnesses.

Other than Jews, by far the largest number of inmates were Poles. At Auschwitz alone, more Poles died than did Romanies, Soviet POWs, and homosexuals at all the other camps combined.

This Soviet POW is identified as Jewish by the yellow badge on his uniform. To be both a Soviet soldier and a Jew was a virtual guarantee that a captive would be quickly executed upon his arrival in a concentration camp.

Chapter 4
The Great Action and Imprisonment

Suddenly, in 1942, the Nazis revealed the true depth of their hatred for Jews and other groups they considered inferior or a threat to a "perfect" German state. Beginning in July, German SS soldiers entered the Warsaw Ghetto and rounded up more than 6,000 people every day. The people were directed to the *Umschlagplatz*, a railroad station that served as a transit point between the ghetto and the outside world. There, soldiers loaded them onto cattle cars on freight trains. The people were told they were heading for a labor camp where Jewish leaders thought conditions might be better. Their true destination, however, was a death camp, where the people were killed by poisonous gas.

An Act of Trust

For the next three months, this terrible roundup, known as the Great Action, occurred daily, until more than 300,000 Jews had been murdered. The inhabitants lived in terror, never knowing which apartment building or city street would be targeted next.

During this period, Irena and her partners were trying to get as many children out as possible. The most difficult part was convincing the parents to give their precious children to strangers. The parents would ask whether Irena was sure that the boy or girl would be safe. Said Irena:

"We had to answer honestly that we could offer no guarantees; I said I couldn't even be certain I would safely leave the Ghetto with a child that very day."

Sometimes Irena would be told to return the following day so the family could make a decision. Action was urgently required, however, and some families and their children had been transported to the death camps by the time Irena returned a second time.

The Umschlagplatz *(German for "hub" or "collection point") in the Warsaw Ghetto. This was a railroad loading stop where Jews were gathered to be deported to Treblinka and other death camps.*

The SS: Brutal Enforcers of Nazi Hatred

The *Schutzstaffel* ("protection squadron"), better known as the SS, was founded in 1925 as a personal bodyguard service for Adolf Hitler. When Hitler became leader of Germany in 1933, the SS expanded into a harsh force of 50,000 members. By the time World War II started in 1939, the SS had grown to five times that number.

Among the better-known SS units were the Gestapo, or secret state police, and the brutal guards in charge of the concentration camps. SS officers were trained to turn a blind eye to human suffering. They were schooled in racial hatred as part of their training to carry out the campaign to exterminate Europe's Jews and other minorities. They also had to prove the racial "purity" of their own lineage back more than 200 years.

Left: the official insignia worn on most SS uniforms. Right: a military hat displaying a traditional emblem adopted by the Nazis—the Totenkopf, *or "death's head." After the war, both the SS and the Nazi Party were outlawed in Germany.*

Zegota—Polish Resistance

Beginning in the fall of 1942, after the Great Action deportations, the Nazis reduced the aid money available and increased security. SS officers checked the identities of those receiving aid so that it was much more difficult for Irena and the other social workers to redirect assistance to Jews. A co-worker told her about a new organization that a secret group of concerned aid workers was starting up. The organization was backed by the Polish resistance inside Poland and by the Polish government-in-exile. They called it the Provisional Committee to Aid Jews, and it was code named *Zegota*. Irena went to see the founders at once, and they appointed her head of the Jewish children's section.

With Irena's network and the funds that Zegota was able to get from Jewish organizations in the United States and from the Polish government-in-exile, there would be a greater chance of success. As she said, "Vast sums passed through my hands and it was a great relief to me when I could prove that the money reached the right place." The money went to families, orphanages, convents, and other groups that were secretly housing Jews. Funds were also used to pay bribes to soldiers and officials so they could help thousands escape. The group members risked their lives to help Jews since the Nazis decreed that these activities were punishable by death.

Members of Zegota, the Polish resistance group that Irena Sendler joined as part of her campaign to rescue Jewish children from certain death at the hands of the Nazis.

> "Some Jewish mothers would spend months preparing their children for the Aryan side. They changed their identities. They would say 'You're not Icek, you're Jacek. And I'm not your mother, I was just the housemaid. You'll go with this lady and perhaps over there your mummy will be waiting for you.'"

Irena Sendler

The public execution of two Polish men accused of aiding Jews in 1943. Often the Nazis wiped out entire villages in Poland as punishment for members of the community hiding or otherwise coming to the aid of Jews. The victims of these reprisals included members of the clergy, their congregations, farmers, peasants, and others, including those whom they were protecting.

This photo of Irena Sendler was taken in 1943-44. At that time, she had escaped from Pawiak Prison in the Warsaw Ghetto. This photo was likely used in papers she had made to conceal her identity.

Jan Karski (1913-2000): Messenger of Doom

The Nazi extermination of the Jews was planned on such a huge scale that it was difficult to imagine in the world outside of Poland. One man risked his life on a secret mission into the Warsaw Ghetto and a concentration camp to witness these atrocities. He then reported back to members of the Polish government-in-exile and to Allied government leaders.

Jan Karski was a Polish diplomat in the late 1930s whose wartime exploits included some death-defying events. While serving with the Polish army during World War II, he was captured by the Soviet Red Army and then handed over to the Germans. He was able to escape, and he joined the Polish underground resistance movement, where he became a courier carrying messages across enemy lines.

In August 1942, he slipped into the Warsaw Ghetto through the cellar of a house on the so-called Aryan side. Resistance workers gave him some ragged clothes and an armband with the Star of David on it, and led him through a tunnel. Irena Sendler recalled that she was one of his guides on this mission, although she didn't know his identity at the time. Once inside, he saw dead bodies in the streets and starving children who were little more than walking skeletons.

Resistance leaders arranged for him to go to the Umschlagplatz transit depot, disguised in a Ukrainian militiaman's uniform. Here he witnessed thousands of Jews being beaten and robbed of their possessions before being pushed into railcars for the journey to the concentration camps.

Armed with what he had witnessed, Jan left Poland for Britain. During the course of this risk-filled journey, he had to take trains through dangerous territory—Germany and Nazi-occupied France—to Spain. There, he was picked up and taken to London. He carried with him a specially designed key. Inside the hollow shaft of this key was microfilm that contained miniature copies of important documents. Before he left Warsaw, he had several teeth removed by a dentist so that his mouth would swell. He did this in case the German authorities questioned him. He thought his slurred speech would cover his Polish accent.

Once in London, Jan met with British officials. He then went to the United States, where he met with President Franklin Roosevelt and other powerful officials. He passed along the urgent pleas of the Jewish resistance leaders, but he wasn't able to convince other countries to help. "Almost every individual was sympathetic to my reports concerning the Jews," he said. "But when I reported to the leaders of governments they discarded their conscience, their personal feeling."

By that time, Polish officials claimed it was too dangerous for him to return, since the Germans knew his identity. He remained in the United States, where he taught at a Washington university for 40 years. He also wrote and lectured against the iron-fisted policies of the Soviet-based communist system that Poland endured in the decades following the end of the war.

> *"This sin will haunt humanity to the end of time. It does haunt me. And I want it to be so."*
>
> Jan Karski

In this photo, taken in 1994 at the United States Holocaust Museum in Washington, D.C., Jan Karski points to a map and talks about his secret missions into the Warsaw Ghetto in 1942.

Everything had to be done with utmost secrecy. Individual couriers and other volunteers who worked with Irena often did not have much knowledge of the details or even what the organization was called.

The Warsaw Ghetto Uprising

By 1943, most of the Warsaw Ghetto population had been wiped out. The district contained a fraction of its former population since the Great Action a few months earlier—the deportation of more than 300,000 Jews to the death camps, where they were killed.

Jewish resistance groups had decided not to fight the deportations because they believed the lie that the people were being resettled in labor camps. When they discovered what was really happening, that people were being killed in large numbers, the remaining residents prepared for one last fight, now known as the Warsaw Ghetto Uprising. The uprising began on January 18, 1943, with the most intense fighting occurring in April and May, when members of the Jewish combat organization and other Jewish civilians greeted the German soldiers with small handguns and improvised bombs. The Germans overpowered the resisters, going from street to street, systematically torching the buildings in the ghetto.

By May 16, 1943, the Nazis had beaten all but a handful of fighters, and the revolt had officially ended. Sporadic fighting continued into June, when the Nazis defeated the last of the fighters. The ghetto lay in ruins, and an estimated 13,000 Jews died during the fighting. The remaining 50,000 were transported to Nazi concentration

and death camps. Most of them were sent to the
Treblinka death camp in eastern Poland.

The Warsaw Ghetto Uprising was the first of
two events during World War II when the city's
citizens planned a violent revolt against the
occupying Nazis. The second, an uprising among
the general populace of Warsaw, took place the
following year. During the Warsaw Ghetto
Uprising, when the Jewish community finally
fought back in desperation after all their horrific
treatment, Irena and her team were banned
from entering the area. They had been able to
help Jews in the ghetto previously by using the
special passes given to health workers. Now,
they could only wait outside and watch carefully
the escape routes such as basements and sewers
in order to help anybody—child or adult—who
was trying to flee.

*The Warsaw
Ghetto lies
in ruins
following its
destruction
by the Nazis
in the
aftermath of
the uprising.*

Jewish resistance fighters following their capture during the Warsaw Ghetto Uprising in 1943. Despite its ultimate failure, the ghetto uprising helped inspire those who planned and fought in the general Warsaw Uprising the following year.

"It is not true that the ghetto martyrs died without putting up a fight. The fight was every day, every hour, every minute, surviving in that hell year after year. When they finally realized there was no more hope for them, they heroically took up arms."

Irena Sendler

Irena's team would arrange for fake identification, new clothes, and a safe place to live. On top of that, she had to continue to check on the children already in hiding and be ready to quickly move them if she sensed they might be discovered.

Caught ...

Even though she had a code name—Jolanta—Irena knew that she and the records she kept of her work were under constant risk of discovery. She was therefore very careful to hide her social work records. The volunteers in Irena's Zegota network also kept notes about the identities of the children they had saved and where they were hidden. The documents would help reunite children with their parents after the war. They had various ways of hiding the notes. If the authorities confiscated the lists, the information would be lost, and the names contained in them might endanger the safety of others, as well.

In 1943, the event Irena had been dreading finally happened. She was at the apartment she

In one of the best-known and most dramatic World War II photographs, a group of Jews is shown being rounded up by the SS following the Warsaw Ghetto Uprising in 1943.

shared with her mother, enjoying a social evening with friends on her name day, which fell on October 20. In Poland people celebrate on the saint's day for whom they were named. The guests stayed overnight because of the curfew law forbidding them from going out on the street after a certain time. Late in the night, she heard a pounding on the door. It was the dreaded Gestapo! Before she let them in, she grabbed her precious lists of names of the hidden children. She was about to throw them out the window, but then she realized the building was surrounded. She quickly tossed the crumpled paper to her trusted friend.

The police spent three hours searching the apartment while the women watched in fear. They ripped open mattresses and pillows, lifted floorboards, and examined possessions. Fortunately, they didn't find the scroll of paper, which Irena's friend had managed to keep hidden under her arm. Nor did they find the fake identification cards and bundles of money Irena had kept under her bed.

... Interrogated ...

Not satisfied, the police took Irena away to be questioned at the infamous Gestapo headquarters at 25 Szucha Avenue. Here, prisoners were subjected to brutal means of interrogation, including beatings and torture.

On the way to the interrogation, Irena was horrified to discover something in the pocket of her jacket. It was another list—this one of children who were to receive money for living expenses the next day. If the police found it, the children and their foster parents would be in danger. She quietly tore up the list into small shreds and secretly pushed them out the window.

The police had gotten her name from the owner of the laundry that was one of Zegota's contact points for the network of underground activists. They had arrested the woman and tortured her. Eventually, unable to hold out any longer, she gave the Gestapo Irena's name and those of several of her colleagues. The interrogator told Irena that if she gave them details about the Zegota organization, she would be released. Subjected to intense interrogation and torture, Irena didn't budge. As she said much later,

"I was silent because I preferred to die rather than reveal our activity. What did my life mean compared with so many other people's lives, lives that I could have endangered?"

Soon she was transferred to an even more fearsome place: Pawiak Prison. Built in the 1800s and taken over by the Nazis when they

Pawiak Prison as it looked during the time that Irena Sendler was held by the Nazis during World War II.

invaded Poland in 1939, Pawiak was actually located in the Warsaw Ghetto. A place of extreme cruelty for Jews and non-Jews alike, Pawiak was the scene of vicious interrogations by the Gestapo, deportations to death camps, and executions on the prison grounds. As soon as Irena arrived at Pawiak, the Nazis placed her in a crowded cell, gave her a gray and black striped uniform, and forced her to work in the prison laundry along with about 20 other women. Their job was scrubbing the soiled underwear of other prisoners and guards. Regularly, the authorities interrogated her and then whipped and beat her when she refused to give any information.

> *"I still carry the marks on my body of what those 'German supermen' did to me then."*
>
> Irena Sendler

... But Not Forgotten

One day, a medical team arrived. The group included prisoners who were doctors, and Irena recognized one of them. The next time they came, they told her to go to the prison dentist. Irena was puzzled because she hadn't complained of a toothache. As it turned out, the appointment was just an ingenious way to pass a secret message. She went, and the dentist drilled a hole in her healthy tooth and inserted in it a tiny note from her compatriots at Zegota. The note told her to stay hopeful. It also let her know that there were people in the prison who were in touch with Zegota and that her friends hadn't forgotten her.

Grim Conditions, Terror, and Death

The prisoners faced a struggle just to stay alive, and they spent much of their energy trying to figure out ways to get enough food to survive on. When women were arrested, some of them were permitted to bring their children with them to jail. Some of the prison jailers were kind to the children, and they sometimes allowed the children to sneak into the cellar to take some extra vegetables stored there. Irena and the others in the laundry had worked out a plan with the children to bring back some potatoes for them as well.

Irena recalled boiling potatoes secretly mixed in with the loads of laundry. The punishment for this and other minor offenses was severe. Occasionally, for example, the guards became angry that the prisoners had scrubbed the underwear so vigorously with brushes that some of the pants had holes in them. One time, they marched into the laundry, lined the workers up, and shot every second woman there. Irena and her fellow workers were horrified.

Irena continued to endure the painful beatings she received, but soon she feared for her life when jailers began a period of mass executions. Every morning, names of the prisoners slated for execution would be called out. One day in January 1944, after she had been in prison for three months, Irena heard her name. She had assumed the day would come when her fate would become the same as the others and she would die here. That day seemed to have arrived. She and a group of more than 30 others were taken to the Gestapo headquarters. There, each person's name was called, and she was told to go into a certain room. Irena's orders were different. Fully convinced that, as she said later, "I was sentenced to death," she was told to go into another room. There, to her shock, a Gestapo man led her to the exit and told her she was free.

Freedom Again

Zegota, the secret agency for which Irena had risked her life, had bribed a Gestapo guard to get her released. He filled out all the proper documents showing that she had been executed. She could hardly believe it. She went to a nearby shop, where the owner gave her a winter coat and some money for the streetcar. Irena had a very brief reunion with her overjoyed mother, Janina, but her courier told her she must go into hiding, since she was supposed to be officially dead. From then on, she would have a new

Janusz Korczak: The Good Doctor and His Orphanage

Born in Warsaw in 1878, Henryk Goldszmit was a Polish Jewish pediatrician and famous children's author. Known by his pen name, Janusz Korczak, he is remembered for how he died as well as how he lived. He wrote several children's fairy tales, including *King Matt the First and Kajtus the Wizard,* and he had a popular radio program in the 1930s. As director of an orphanage for Jewish children, he created a setting that empowered his young brood, encouraging them to create their own newspaper, government, and court.

Janusz Korczak.

When the Nazis occupied Poland, they moved his orphanage into the Warsaw Ghetto. The man whom the children called Pan Doktor (Mr. Doctor) was forced to move the orphanage twice as the boundaries of the ghetto shrank. Finally, in August 1942, the Nazis ordered the orphanage's children and staff to march to the train station. From there, they were to be deported to the Treblinka concentration camp. Reportedly offered several chances to be smuggled out of the ghetto to the so-called Aryan side, Koraczak refused to abandon his children to their fate.

Irena Sendler was one of the witnesses that day who saw the Doctor walking with his children and staff to their deaths. By all accounts they were quiet and happy, dressed in their best clothes. Said Irena, "I saw that tragic parade in the street, those innocent children walking obediently in the procession of death and listening to the doctor's optimistic words. I do not know why for me and for all the other eyewitnesses our hearts did not break."

A memorial in Warsaw to Janusz Korczak and the children under his care.

The graffiti "Pawiak pomscimy," which means "Pawiak will be avenged" in English, was scrawled by a Polish resistance fighter in Warsaw. It refers to the mass executions of the prison's inmates by the Nazis.

identity with fake papers and lead a life of hiding, just like the people she had helped.

In the meantime, her mother's heart condition had grown worse, and Irena spent the days with her and the nights at a neighbor's apartment. The Gestapo knew that Janina was Irena's mother, and when they started asking around about Janina, Irena called on doctor friends to have her moved by ambulance to a safer location in another friend's apartment, where they could both live. Eventually, two months after Irena had gained her freedom from Pawiak Prison, Janina passed away. Irena couldn't even attend the funeral for fear of being arrested again.

Back to Work

After her mother's death, and with less than a year until the end of the war, Irena turned all her attention to her Zegota activities. She couldn't contact her old employer, the city of Warsaw, and her husband was in a POW camp. Her valuable and dangerous work was her first priority. It was up to her to deliver money to support families where an activist had been arrested. She also delivered medicine and other valuable commodities to secret drop points.

Irena continued to check on the welfare of the children her team had managed to smuggle out of the ghetto before it was liquidated, or destroyed. These children were living in emergency shelters, convents, or foster homes operated by a network of trusted associates. Catholic priests and nuns and contacts within the civil service could provide phony baptism papers and other identification. Members of Zegota made frequent checks on the hidden children and treated them with special attention to ease their fears. The children had to memorize their new identities. They were also taught to speak Polish and recite some Catholic prayers and nursery rhymes so they could fool the German officers if they were questioned.

"In the season of great dying, Irena Sendler dedicated her entire life to saving Jews."

Michal Glowinski, Polish professor who was saved by Irena during World War II when he was eight years old

Making sure the Jewish children didn't stand out in a crowd was very important if the day came when they had to be seen in public while shifting to new locations. One of Irena's young Zegota volunteers used to take groups of Jewish children outdoors to play. The children had grown pale from months of hiding indoors, so swimming and playing helped give them back some normal color.

This photo appears in a book about an order of Polish nuns who are reported to have helped save 20 Jewish children by taking them into their care, teaching them Catholic prayers and customs, and hiding them among non-Jewish children at their boarding school. Of the seven girls pictured here, two are Christian and the other five are from Jewish families. These girls were fortunate that their parents, assimilated Jews whose clothing and demeanor were similar to those of non-Jewish Poles, were able to visit them during the war.

"Although so many years have passed since these tragic events, there are nights when in my troubled dreams I still hear the weeping, the cries of despair, the terrifying sobs."

Irena Sendler

HEROES OF THE HOLOCAUST: THE SECRET SAVIOR

The stories of the Holocaust reveal humans at their worst. During this time of great oppression and cruelty, however, there were many tales of bravery and compassion on the part of non-Jews. Irena Sendler is one of those outstanding heroines. Here and on the pages following are portraits of some others who acted to support their fellow humans in the face of grave danger.

Sir Nicholas Winton is a British humanitarian—a person concerned with the welfare of others. His parents, of German Jewish origin, had moved to Britain. There, they converted to Christianity, and when Nicholas was born, he, too, was baptized as a Christian. During the 1930s, he was a stockbroker planning a ski vacation in Switzerland. Instead, he traveled to Czechoslovakia to visit a friend in Prague (now the capital of the Czech Republic) who was doing refugee work with Jews.

The British government had just approved a law permitting youths under 17 years old to stay in Britain provided they had a place to stay. So while in Prague, Winton set up an aid program and advertised for British homeowners willing to take in children. He found homes for almost 700 Jewish children, many of whose parents later died in the Auschwitz concentration camp.

Winton served in the British Royal Air Force during World War II and kept quiet about his aid work. It was only in the 1980s, after his wife found his scrapbooks with lists of names, that his role became public. He was knighted in 2002 by the British monarchy.

Sir Nicholas Winton in 2008.

HEROES OF THE HOLOCAUST: HIDING IN PLAIN SIGHT

One of the key members of the network of "co-conspirators" working with Irena to save lives was a woman named Jadwiga Piotrowska. With other members of her family, including her parents and her daughter, Piotrowska participated in the campaign to rescue and protect Jews during World War II. Their home at 9 Lekarska Street in Warsaw was a beehive of underground activity and a type of emergency care center for Jewish children who were being hidden from the Nazis. There they could be calmed, clothed and fed, and taught to speak some Polish and to say Catholic prayers while they were waiting for papers and places in foster homes, convents, and orphanages.

In back of Piotrowska's home there were garden plots and an apple tree, where, for a while, Piotrowska buried records of the hidden children in a soda bottle. The house was located right across the street from a German encampment and hospital, but it had entrances and exits on two separate streets. Piotrowska often said that is why they were never caught. She would go in one entrance dressed as one person and, dressed as someone else, take adults and children out the other.

In this photo, taken just before World War II began, Jadwiga Piotrowska is shown walking on a street in Warsaw with her parents (left) and her daughter Hana. During the German occupation of Poland, all of Jadwiga's family helped Jewish children who faced certain death at the hands of the Nazis.

HEROES OF THE HOLOCAUST:
GIVING HOPE TO THE HOPELESS

Julian Grobelny was one of the founders of Zegota, the council formed in 1942 to aid Jews. He and his wife Halina turned their tiny house into a temporary shelter for Jews fleeing the Warsaw Ghetto. From their home, they created fake "Aryan" papers and provided escapees with money and medical care. They also worked with Irena to smuggle children out. Grobelny was listed as an enemy of Nazi Germany because of his years of work as an activist in the Polish Socialist Party.

Julian Grobelny, as photographed sometime in the 1930s.

It was for activism unrelated to his rescuing Jews that Grobelny was arrested by the Gestapo in 1944. Thanks to the help of physician friends in prison, he was able to survive his imprisonment, despite his poor health from tuberculosis. After the war, he became mayor of a town in central Poland, and he died there of tuberculosis in 1946.

In 1987, Julian and Halina Grobelny were given the title "Righteous among the Nations" by Israel's official Holocaust memorial, Yad Vashem.

HEROES OF THE HOLOCAUST:
RESCUER OF THOUSANDS

As a Swiss diplomat in Hungary during the war, Carl Lutz lent his services to the Jewish Agency for Palestine, creating documents to allow 10,000 Hungarian Jewish children to emigrate. Using his negotiating skills, he got permission to create thousands of official letters offering Swiss protection for thousands of Jews so they could travel to Palestine (present-day Israel). He also set up 76 houses that could not be raided under diplomatic immunity rules. Altogether, he is believed to have saved more than 60,000 Jews. In 1964, Yad Vashem, Israel's official Holocaust memorial, named Lutz one of the "Righteous among the Nations."

Chapter 5
Warsaw Uprising and Liberation

In 1944, nearly five long years since Hitler's invasion of Poland, the tide of the war seemed to be turning toward the Allies and against Nazi Germany and the other Axis nations. The Germans were in retreat, and the Soviet Union's Red Army was approaching Warsaw after sweeping across Eastern Europe. The Nazis had brutally put down the Warsaw Ghetto Uprising a year earlier. Soviet troops—who were fighting with the Allies—were only about 10 miles (16 kilometers) away. Poland's underground resistance movement, called *Armia Krajowa*, which in English means "the Home Army," believed the time was right to try to drive the Germans from the city.

A Final Stand

On August 1, 1944, Polish Home Army General Tadeusz Komorowski, acting under orders of the Polish government-in-exile in Britain, gave the command to start fighting. Fighting in the streets rather than on a battlefield, the outnumbered Polish insurgents were able to gain some ground and capture such key positions as the gas, electric, and water services for the city.

The resistance fighters had assumed the Allies would help. The Soviet army—which was

General Tadeusz Komorowski directed Polish resistance forces in the Warsaw Uprising of 1944. His hope—and that of the Polish government-in-exile—was that the Polish Home Army would liberate Warsaw from the Nazis. This would have prevented advancing Soviet forces from taking control of Poland at the end of World War II. The Germans crushed the uprising, however, and the Soviets would officially liberate Poland in January 1945.

in the closest position of the Allied armies—did not move in to offer military support, however. Instead, Red Army troops waited outside the city. By doing so, the Soviets prevented the Polish Home Army from leading a victory over the Nazis. A Polish-led victory would have allowed the Polish government-in-exile to return to Warsaw from London. That would have made Poland a free, democratic nation. Instead, as it had for years, the Soviet Union, under dictator Joseph Stalin, had its own plans for Poland.

Now, with the end of the war closer than ever, those plans would include the Red Army liberating Poland from the Nazis. Poland would then come under the military control of the Soviet forces. In the aftermath of the war, Poland became a nation governed by a Soviet-style communist regime and remained under Soviet domination for decades.

Giving Help Where Needed

The uprising in Warsaw lasted an incredible 63 days before it was crushed by the Germans. The British Royal Air Force sent more than 200 air drops of military weaponry and other supplies,

and the United States provided some support later in the campaign. The bombing and destruction of many of the buildings left Polish civilians homeless and impoverished.

During the Warsaw Uprising, Irena continued to make a valuable contribution. She had some Red Cross training in nursing, and she joined a small clinic to treat the wounded. At one point, the medical team moved into an empty house where they surprised a German soldier, who stabbed her in the leg with a bayonet. The wound became infected and endangered her life, but she received good care from her friends despite the poor conditions.

Irena participated in many dramatic medical interventions. These included an operation

Joseph Stalin: Ruthless Tyrant

Joseph Stalin, the leader of the Soviet Union during World War II, was born in 1879 in Georgia—then part of the Russian Empire, later a part of the Soviet Union, and now an independent republic. The son of a cobbler, he joined the revolutionaries fighting against the Russian monarchy in the early 1900s and was arrested several times. In 1922, following the birth of the Soviet Union out of Russia, Ukraine, Belarus, and other formerly independent nations, Stalin became General Secretary of the Communist Party. After the death of Soviet leader Vladimir Lenin in 1924, Stalin became the undisputed head of the Soviet Union.

Stalin forced small famers to join large agricultural collectives, and he dramatically increased industrial production. He was ruthless against any groups he considered a threat, even his own citizens. Historians hold him responsible for executing millions and exiling millions more to remote labor camps as a part of his campaign to strengthen his rule as well as his economic and political policies. He is also blamed for a terrible famine in wheat-growing Soviet Ukraine in the 1930s that also killed many more.

Stalin signed a secret "non-aggression pact" with Adolf Hitler in 1939. This meant that Germany and the Soviet Union would not attack each other, and they each took over part of Poland at the beginning of World War II. When Germany broke the agreement and attacked the Soviet Union in 1941, Stalin joined the United States, Canada, Britain, and other Allied nations. During the war, he met with the other "Big Three" Allied leaders (shown below, left to right: Stalin, U.S. President Franklin D. Roosevelt, and British Prime Minister Winston Churchill). He successfully argued that his country should have continued control over the smaller countries he had occupied, such as Poland. As a result of this agreement, most Eastern Europe nations were run by governments dominated by Soviet-style communists.

Under Stalin, the Soviet Union paid a high price for defeating the Germans. Historians estimated 30 million Soviet soldiers died and as many as 20 million civilians perished during the conflict. Stalin died in 1953.

Liberated Jewish women pose with Polish Home Army resistance fighters in August 1944. The fighters had just freed these and several hundred other inmates from a Warsaw prison that the Nazis had turned into a concentration camp. The camp was connected to the infamous Pawiak Prison. Following their liberation, many of the former inmates joined the Warsaw Uprising.

A Polish soldier is captured in September 1944 by German troops who discovered him beneath a manhole cover during the Warsaw Uprising.

performed with kitchen knives—and without anesthetic—on a bombing victim who had lost an arm. As the Germans regained the upper hand during the uprising, they evacuated whole neighborhoods of civilians, many of them engaged in the fight. Irena and her team were relocated to a former marmalade factory. There, they continued to help the sick and wounded.

Liberation

In 1944, despite the defeat of the Polish resistance in Warsaw, the German forces were gradually being overpowered. Soviet Red Army soldiers surged against the enemy to drive them out of their country. As the Soviets pushed the Germans back aross Poland, Czechoslovakia, and Romania, they made some horrifying discoveries—gas chambers and

Irena put her training as a nurse with the Red Cross to use during the Warsaw Uprising in 1944.

Warsaw residents greet members of the Soviet Red Army and the Polish Home Army on January 17, 1945, the day Warsaw was liberated from the Nazis.

crematories where bodies were burned and still-living but starving prisoners. The Allies had known for some time that these mass killings were going on. The liberation of the Majdanek concentration camp in Lublin, Poland, in July 1944, however, marked the first time they could see it with their own eyes. In January 1945, the Soviets marched into the ruins of Warsaw and officially liberated it from its German occupiers. January 17 is still celebrated in Poland today as Liberation Day.

Despite the joy the citizens felt at being free at last, and out from under the Nazi oppression, it was still a time of severe poverty and hunger for many. At the time of liberation, Irena was working in an orphanage that was a converted hospital. The change in government meant the orphanage was short of food and financing. Irena spoke to her old colleagues and was able to secure some much-needed funding. Work went on amid the chaos and the ruins.

Soviet soldiers stand before the crematorium ovens at Majdanek, the first concentration camp to be viewed firsthand by Allied forces, in the summer of 1944. The Nazis tried to dismantle the camp before the advancing Red Army arrived to liberate it, but were only partially successful in tearing down these ovens.

WARSAW REBUILT

Warsaw, a city with a metropolitan population of close to three million people, contains famous churches and palaces, some designed as early as the 1300s. While they may look old to visitors, the buildings are actually quite new, as they were rebuilt since World War II ended. The city was damaged badly during the invasion of Poland in 1939. Then, after the Warsaw Uprising in 1944, Nazi soldiers systematically demolished the city, destroying eight out of every ten buildings.

Now Warsaw is on the United Nation's list of World Heritage Sites as an example of an outstanding reconstruction of 13th–20th century architecture.

Scenes typical of Warsaw then and now. Below right: The ruins of Warsaw's historic Old Town Market Place in 1945, after the Nazis blew it up following the Warsaw Uprising. Inset: The Market Place today, rebuilt to look the way it did from the time of its original design in the 1600s until World War II.

Above left: One feature of rebuilt Warsaw is a statue called the Maly Powstaniec, or "Little Insurgent." The statue is of a small boy carrying a gun. He represents the youthful fighters who bravely struggled for freedom during the Warsaw Uprising.

Self-Sacrifice and Survival

Katarzyna Meloch's mother, Wanda, a well-known Polish Jewish writer and activist, was executed by the Nazis in the city of Bialystock in 1941. Before her death, Wanda had taught nine-year-old Katarzyna how to reach her uncle (Wanda's brother) in the Warsaw Ghetto.

When Katarzyna made it to Warsaw, she stayed in the ghetto until it was no longer safe. That is when a young Polish woman named Jadwiga Deneka smuggled her over to the "Aryan" side. Jadwiga, a Zegota member and associate of Irena Sendler, had been a student of Katarzyna's mother and had lost her own child in the bombing of Warsaw. Jadwiga took special care of Katarzyna, protecting the young girl in her home, obtaining a birth certificate for her with the name of a Polish girl on it, and moving her to a remote convent in Turkowice. There, the nuns, at great risk to themselves, protected Katarzyna and other Jewish children by placing them among the convent's non-Jewish orphans.

Jadwiga Deneka sent Katarzyna packages at the convent and continued to be concerned about her. The Germans eventually captured Jadwiga. Tortured at Pawiak Prison, she wrote to friends that she was ready to die for her cause. In 1943, the Germans shot her with a group of Jewish women.

Thanks to the selfless courage of Jadwiga Deneka and the nuns at Turkowice, Katarzyna survived the war. Today she is a journalist in Warsaw who writes about the heroism of others and about her experience of living with a dual identity during and after the war.

Top to bottom: Katarzyna Meloch's mother and uncle, 1924; Katarzyna (on left with two ribbons in hair) with other children at Turkowice convent; Jadwiga Denek; Katarzyna in a recent photo.

Chapter 6
Postwar and Legacy

In May 1945, Germany surrendered and the guns were finally silenced. The war in Europe was over. Throughout Europe, people who had lived in fear as battles raged around them were left to do what they could to move on with their lives. Declaring an end to war did not, however, solve the enormous social, political, and economic problems faced by nations and individuals alike.

People Without Countries

Millions of citizens were displaced persons. This meant that they were people without countries, having been forced to migrate away from their homes. Many had been driven out or

The defeat of Germany in World War II rarely brought instant relief to the victims of Nazi aggression. When Allied forces liberated the concentration camps, many of the inmates who were still alive were sick or starving and close to death, and they needed medical attention to survive. In this photo, a man breaks down and weeps when he learns that he will not be in the first group of inmates sent by the U.S. Army to a hospital for treatment.

A worn-looking ID photo of Irena taken during the war.

fled because of ethnic or religious persecution. Many had been prisoners in camps or had survived forced marches to new locations. Many were children who had been separated from their parents and relatives. In some cases, their countries had changed dramatically while they had been away, and they were unable, or did not wish, to return.

European nations that had joined the Axis forces—or that Germany had invaded and controlled—now fell under control of Allied nations. At first, Allied countries ran camps to shelter and feed these people, and then the United Nations took over operating these facilities. Eventually, Poland and other nations, most of them in Eastern Europe, fell into the orbit of the Soviet Union and were placed under communist rule.

Poland's Postwar Challenge

In 1945, even though Warsaw and the rest of Poland were finally free of Nazi occupation, it was still an immense challenge to live in the ruined city, much of it destroyed by fire or

For this Polish girl, shown grieving over the body of her older sister, the end of the war meant facing a life that would never return to normal. The older girl was killed by machine gun fire from low-flying Nazi aircraft that had returned for a second pass over her family's farm.

This photo dramatically shows the extent of destruction in the wake of the Nazi occupation of Warsaw. With over 80 percent of the buildings damaged or destroyed, people returning to the city—and those who, like Irena, had been in Warsaw throughout the war—often had to live in cellars or out in the open.

explosives at the hands of the enemy. What would people eat? Where would they sleep? How would they survive? Answering these questions was a social worker's nightmare. Irena took the job of head of the Warsaw Health and Welfare Department just as thousands of destitute people were returning to the city from hiding places in foster homes or convents. Some resistance fighters had hidden in the forest. "We worked day and night, hungry and cold, living like others returning to Warsaw, in basements, frequently with rats for company," said Irena.

Ten days after Soviet troops liberated Warsaw, they reached the Auschwitz concentration camp, where they rescued about 7,000 prisoners, including many children. Irena assisted with orphaned children who arrived in Warsaw from the camps. Not only did they urgently require medical care and food, but they also needed intensive love and attention. The children had witnessed horrible events, and they were malnourished and infested with lice.

Survivors of the Auschwitz-Birkenau death camp peer out from behind barbed wire during the camp's liberation by the Soviet Red Army in 1945.

Finding the Children

Irena and her friends had kept careful records of the names and new homes of the children they had helped save. They hid these records in ovens, behind walls, under floorboards, and in other places. After the war, most of the children were tracked down and located, and a local group arranged reunions for the children with parents who had survived. Sometimes the reunions were painful for those who had grown to love their new families. Some of the younger children who had been hiding for several years had known only their foster family and did not remember their own blood relatives. Many children whose families had died were placed in orphanages and later sent to Palestine (present-day Israel).

Irena's Own Children

The war had delayed Irena's plans for her own family life, and adjusting to the postwar lifestyle was tumultuous. Her husband had survived the war despite his imprisonment, but they decided to divorce soon after. In 1947, she married lawyer and social activist Stefan Zgrzembski, whom she had worked with in the resistance movement. They had three children—Janina, born in 1947; Andrzej, born in 1949 (who lived for 11 days); and Adam, born in 1951 (who died in 1999). Irena's second marriage ended in a separation. Irena also had two foster children—Teresa and Irenka—whose own families had been killed. They lived with her while they completed schooling after the war.

Although the Nazi occupation of Poland had ended, the country was now occupied by the Soviet Union, which established a communist regime. While conditions improved dramatically over how things had been under the Nazis, the new government imposed restrictions on personal freedom and controlled the economy. Politicians were not democratically elected by the people. The government also took control of the Catholic Church and harassed members of the clergy in this largely Catholic country.

Viewed today as a World War II heroine who

After the war, survivors of the Holocaust attempted to become reunited with loved ones from whom they'd been separated. Many found new lives far away from where they'd been persecuted. These two survivors, one an eight-year old boy, are shown as they arrived by boat in Haifa, Palestine (now Israel), just after the surrender of Nazi Germany in 1945.

WORLD MEMORY PROJECT

Even today, many years after the war, families continue to discover new facts about their lost relatives. In May 2011, the United States Holocaust Memorial Museum partnered with Ancestry.com to create the World Memory Project. This is planned to be the world's largest free online database of information on victims of Nazi persecution during World War II (www.worldmemoryproject.org). The website has millions of pages of digitized records and information on about 17 million people. It provides a very valuable archive for historians as well as people searching for details about their family members.

saved lives and brought families back together, Irena was seen as a potential threat by the harsh government of postwar Poland. Raising her own children in communist Poland proved difficult, since they faced prejudice because of their mother's work. When Irena's children began their university education, both of them suffered harassment from officials.

Struggling to Keep Up the Good Fight

In Warsaw's Welfare Department, Irena could see that postwar society under the new government was a different place, a place where politics came first. In the past, she had always supported Polish socialist groups. To her, socialism meant compassion and support for others. In 1948, the group to which Irena belonged, the Polish Socialist Party, merged with the Polish Workers' Party to form the Polish United Workers' Party, which became the country's ruling communist party.

With the party no longer representing the socialist ideals she had supported, Irena handed in her membership book. As a result, she was threatened and shunned. She narrowly avoided being arrested for her beliefs, saved by a friend whose husband was in charge of security. The friend begged her husband not to arrest Irena because Irena had saved her life by hiding her during the war.

After a few years, Irena left the Welfare Department to join the Ministry of Education, and later the Ministry of Health. There, her job was to oversee the teaching of instructors in such health-related fields as nursing, dentistry, and pharmacy. Around 1967, events in the Middle East touched off a flurry of anti-Semitism in countries with communist governments. Irena believed her political opinions regarding Israel and its Arab neighbors got her in trouble with her employers. Accused of supporting the Jewish state's victory in the 1967 Arab-Israeli War, Irena lost her government job. Not wanting to lose contact with youth, she chose to continue working in education, this time in a school library.

Irena's passion for social work always extended beyond her regular job, and she took on volunteer work. She served on a committee

In this photo taken in 1945 or 1946, a U.S. charity worker is shown providing food and friendly conversation to a three-year-old Jewish girl at a center for displaced persons in Austria.

THE BIRTH OF ISRAEL

In 1948, the state of Israel was created on the very soil that Jews had left nearly 2,000 years earlier. Then, Jewish tribes living in ancient Palestine were exiled while the land was under Roman rule. Now, in the shadow of the Holocaust, Jews in communities all over the world would finally have the homeland they had sought for so long.

Creating a country took years to achieve. The Zionist movement, or support for an independent Jewish homeland, grew strong in the early 1900s. Many Jewish families settled in the Middle East near Jerusalem, a city that is holy to Jews, Christians, and Muslims alike.

Many Jewish soldiers fought in the British Army during World War I. The British succeeded against the Ottoman Turks in winning control of Palestine. At the time, this was an area that included parts of present-day Iraq, Saudi Arabia, Jordan, Israel, and the Palestinian territories.

When World War I was settled in 1918, the British government received control, known as the British Mandate, of Palestine. For a time after the war, the British spoke with Zionist groups and leaders of Arab nations about a plan to support both an Arab and a Jewish entity in Palestine. Palestinian Arabs were not included in the discussions, however, and for decades relations worsened between Arabs, Jews, and British military authorities in Palestine.

Meanwhile, Jewish settlement in Palestine increased steadily, especially in the years leading up to World War II as the persecution of Jews grew stronger in other lands. After World War II, faced with a crisis on both the Arab and Jewish fronts in Palestine, Britain tried to restrict the immigration of Jews, turning away many and placing others in detention camps. In 1947, Britain declared its intention to withdraw from Palestine, stating that it was unable to reach a solution that would be acceptable to Arabs and Jews alike.

In that same year, the United Nations Special Committee on Palestine recommended the land be partitioned, or divided, into two states—one Jewish and the other Arab. The Jewish community of Palestine accepted the plan, but Arab nations rejected it.

On May 14, 1948, the day before the British Mandate expired, Jewish organizations in Palestine proclaimed independence, naming the new country Israel. After Israel declared its independence, the British left the region. The Arabs refused to recognize the Jewish state, and the day after Israeli independence, armies from four neighboring Arab states attacked Israel. After a year of fighting, a cease fire was declared. This truce created borders that shaped most of present-day Israel and the Palestinian territories. The original partition plan was no longer in effect, and hundreds of thousands of Palestinian Arabs either fled or were pressured into leaving during the conflict.

Since then, Israel has signed peace treaties with two of its Arab neighbors, Jordan and Egypt. Relations between Israel and the Arab world at large, however, are still generally unsettled, and territorial battles continue between Israelis and Palestinians to this day.

In these photos, taken in 1920, British security forces are shown checking Jewish (left) and Arab (right) civilians in Jerusalem. Arab anger over increased Jewish immigration to Palestine (present-day Israel), and the failure of British authorities to control violence over the situation, created tensions among the three groups that would only worsen in the decades to come.

for the Polish Red Cross, and she helped found the League for the Struggle Against Racism. Working for groups like these kept her busy even after her retirement from the work force in the 1980s.

Poland Struggles for Democracy

Harsh conditions in communist-run Poland started to change in 1978, when a Polish priest—the Archbishop of Krakow—became Pope John Paul II. To many Catholics in Poland, he was an inspiration. His speeches helped strengthen the movement in Poland against the communist system.

The Solidarity trade union was another force that helped fuel anti-communist sentiment

After World War II, Eastern Europe's communist governments tightly controlled prices and the quantities of goods available to consumers. One result of the uncertainty over what might be available and for how much was long bread lines, like this one in Poland in the 1960s.

> *"The evil of the 20th century was of gigantic proportions, an evil that used state structures to carry out its dirty work; it was evil transformed into a system."*
>
> Pope John Paul II

in Poland. Solidarity started in the Polish shipyards in Gdansk. The group inspired pro-democracy movements in other communist nations in Eastern Europe, including the Soviet Union. Its leaders organized strikes and called for political change. The Polish government finally agreed to hold elections in 1989, and Solidarity won an overwhelming victory in the first democratic government since World War II. Like many Poles, Irena was enthusiastic about the new Solidarity trade union that was challenging the communist regime. She left the Polish Teachers' Union and joined up, inspiring other staffers to do the same thing.

Top Right: Pope John Paul II is shown during a trip to his native land of Poland in 1987. Lech Walesa (right) was the leader of the Solidarity trade union movement that played a major role in bringing Poland to democracy in the late 1980s. Walesa credited the Pope with giving Poles the courage to insist on change. Walesa went on to become Poland's first democratically elected president, serving between 1990 and 1995.

> *"In saving the lives of Jewish children during World War II, Irena Sendler won her own personal struggle against evil, against the heartless cruelty of the outside world. She became a symbol of goodness, love and tolerance."*
>
> Anna Mieszkowska, author of Irena's Polish biography

Irena's Achievements Recognized

Irena's good works were first recognized in the 1960s when Israel's official Holocaust memorial, Yad Vashem, named her one of the "Righteous among the Nations," a title given to gentiles who perform brave deeds in support of Jews. In Poland's strict communist society, however, she wasn't permitted to travel to receive the award. It wasn't until later that the world became aware of her achievements and bravery. She received the award in 1983, and in 1991 she was made an honorary citizen of Israel.

In 1999, some high school students from rural Kansas were looking for a topic for a history project. They researched Irena's activities during World War II and created a play that dramatized her good works. The play, called *Life in a Jar*, is named after a jar in which it was believed, at the time, Irena had sealed the names of Jewish children she had helped escape. Although that specific detail may have been exaggerated over time, the play had an impact on those who learned of it. A project, called Life in a Jar: The Irena Sendler Project, was built around the play. From this project an idea grew for a foundation—the Irena Sendler *Life in a Jar* Foundation—that encourages teachers to tell their students about tolerance through studying heroes such as Irena.

Before her death in 2008, Irena sometimes expressed regret that those with whom she worked hadn't lived long enough to receive the same recognition for their courageous deeds as she had for hers. In this photo, taken sometime after the Warsaw Uprising in 1944, we see some of those people gathered in what is believed to be a medical unit set up in Warsaw to help people displaced by the Germans following the failed Uprising. Seated to the left of Irena is Julian Grobelny, one of the founders of Zegota, the council to aid Jews. To his left is Dr. Maria Skokowska-Rudolf, another one of Irena's medical co-workers from the Uprising. Standing to Irena's right is Stefan Zgrzembski, a lawyer and social activist with whom Irena had worked in the resistance. In 1947, following the end of Irena's marriage to Mieczyslaw Sendler, Irena and Stefan became married.

A Conspiracy of Courage

In 2011, a documentary aired on the Public Broadcasting Service (PBS) entitled Irena Sendler: In the Name of Their Mothers (DVD cover shown here). Along with photographs and news films, much of them disturbing in their frank depiction of life and death in Warsaw during World War II, the documentary features interviews with Irena shortly before her death in 2008. It also includes moving testimonials from some of the now-grown "children" she had rescued from the Warsaw Ghetto.

Importantly, the documentary has also helped bring into public view many of the people who had worked with Irena to rescue children during the war. Most of those people have passed away, but here, in addition to those shown elsewhere in this book, is a look at just some of Irena's many "co-conspirators" who took incredible measures to save the lives of others.

Top row, left to right: Irena Schultz, who smuggled thousands of doses of typhoid medicine into the ghetto; Maria Kukulska (left) and daughter Hanka (right), both workers for Zegota; Jadwiga Petrovska and Jan Dobraczynski, co-workers at the Social Welfare Department. Left: Polish writer, resistance fighter, and Zegota co-founder Zofia Kossak, shown with daughter Anna, who also helped to save children.

More Recognition

Publicity from *Life in a Jar* brought added recognition to Irena and her deeds. In 2003, the Polish government gave Irena the Order of the White Eagle, Poland's highest honor for civilians. In 2007, the Polish Senate honored her with a special resolution. She had a school in Bavaria, Germany, named after her. She also received a letter from the Pope. In 2003, she received the Jan Karski Award, named after the Polish activist. The presentation was made in Washington, and since Irena could not attend, Elzbieta Ficowska accepted it on her behalf. Elzbieta was the baby in the toolbox whom Irena's group had saved from the Warsaw Ghetto so many years ago.

One of the greatest rewards for Irena has been hearing from the children—now adults—she saved. Many have contacted her through various Holocaust survivor organizations—sometimes years afterward, since the trauma

Left: On February 15, 2005, Irena (seated and wearing a black dress) celebrates her 95th birthday. She is joined by a group of family and "children" she rescued during World War II. Notable among her guests is Elzbieta Ficowska (wearing a long scarf), who was the baby smuggled out of the Warsaw Ghetto in a toolbox in 1942. Above: A photo of Elzbieta taken during the war.

for many was extreme. Often, the survivors' own spouses and children were not aware of the history, the tragedy, and the fear of leaving an old life behind and taking on a new identity. In recent times, since the *Life in a Jar* project, Irena's story has been retold in many different ways, adding to her fame. In 2004, a biography of Irena—*Irena Sendler: Mother of the Children of the Holocaust*—was published in Poland. Written by Polish author Anna Mieszkowska, the book was released in English in 2011.

After witnessing some of the worst tragedy and cruelty suffered by humanity, Irena was rewarded with a long life and a quiet death. She died in 2008, quietly and peacefully at the age of 98 in her nursing home while visiting with a friend.

Irena's Legacy and Gift

Following her death, Irena continues to be honored, and her inspiring story continues to be retold. In 2009, she won a humanitarian award from the Audrey Hepburn Foundation. Also in 2009, a television movie starring Anna Paquin, *The Courageous Heart of Irena Sendler*, was released. Irena's deeds are recorded by organizations and memorials dedicated to

"Poland is engaged in a process of deep, difficult and honest soul-searching. We have been blessed for so many years to have her as an example."

Michael Schudrick, Chief Rabbi of Poland, at Irena Sendler's funeral in 2008

remembering the Holocaust. These institutions include the United States Holocaust Memorial Museum in Washington, D.C., which has received more than 30 million visitors since its opening in 1993.

Irena's great gift was her clear-minded decision to do what was right even when these choices put her safety at risk. In addition to her compassionate nature, she was a very skilled planner and organizer. Said Michal Glowinski, one of the children she saved, "In order to rescue children in such terrible circumstances, good intentions were not enough."

The world is not yet free of intolerance, violence, and hate toward people different from ourselves. That's why we will always need many more people like Irena Sendler. Her story makes the reader wonder, "Would I do the same thing in that situation?" After hearing the story of Irena Sendler, one can only hope the answer must be "yes."

Chronology

1910 Irena Krzyzanowska is born in Otwock, in what is now Poland.

1917 Irena's father Stanislaw dies.

1927 Irena begins her studies at the University of Warsaw.

1931 Irena marries Mieczyslaw Sendler.

1932 Irena gets her first professional job, for the Mother and Child Aid Society.

1933 Hitler and the Nazi Party come to power in Germany.

1935 The Mother and Child Aid Society closes, and Irena begins work for the Warsaw Social Welfare Department.

1938 *Kristallnacht,* a widespread pogrom directed against Jews, occurs in Germany and Austria.

1938–1939 *Kindertransport* group rescues 10,000 Jewish children and takes them to Britain.

1939 Hitler invades Poland, and World War II begins. Irena begins volunteering for the Polish Socialist Party due to increasingly harsh decrees against Jews.

1940 The Nazis seal off the Warsaw Ghetto with walls topped with glass and barbed wire.

December 7, 1941 Japan bombs Pearl Harbor, Hawaii. The United States enters World War II.

1942 The Nazis' Great Action begins with mass deportations of Jews to concentration camps. Zegota is established to aid Jews in Poland.

1943 Irena is appointed head of Zegota's section for the care of Jewish children. The Warsaw Ghetto Uprising is launched and crushed by the Nazis. Irena is tracked down by Gestapo, arrested, and sent to Pawiak Prison.

1944 Irena escapes from prison. Her mother Janina dies. Irena assists with a medical team during the Warsaw Uprising.

1945 Warsaw is liberated by the Soviets. In May, the war ends in Europe. In August, the war in the Pacific ends. Irena begins work with Warsaw's Health and Welfare Department.

1947 Following the end of her marriage to Mieczyslaw Sendler, Irena marries Stefan Zgrzembski. Their daughter Janina is born.

1948 State of Israel is established in former British-governed Palestine.

1951 Irena's son Adam is born.

1965 Irena is recognized by Israel's official Holocaust memorial, Yad Vashem, as one of the "Righteous among the Nations."

1967 Irena is fired from her job for pro-Israeli sentiment and begins a new job in a school library.

1983 Irena receives her "Righteous among the Nations" award.

1989 After about a decade of labor unrest and the formation of the trade union Solidarity, the first free and democratic elections in decades are held in Poland.

1991 Irena is made an honorary citizen of Israel.

1999 Irena's son Adam dies.

1999–2000 High school students write a play about Irena.

2003 Irena receives Poland's highest civilian honor, the Order of the White Eagle. She also receives a personal note from Pope John Paul II thanking her for her efforts and wins the Jan Karski Award for her humanitarian deeds.

2004 A biography of Irena, *Irena Sendler: Mother of the Children of the Holocaust*, by Polish author Anna Mieszkowska, is published .

2007 Irena is honored by the Polish Senate.

2008 Irena dies in Poland aged 98.

2009 The TV movie *The Courageous Heart of Irena Sendler* is released.

2011 PBS documentary *Irena Sendler: In the Name of Their Mothers* is released.

Glossary

activist A person who believes in a cause, issue, or political system, and acts to promote that belief.

Allies The countries that fought against Nazi Germany—for example, the United States, Soviet Union, Canada, and Britain.

anti-Semitism Suspicion, hatred, or prejudice directed at Jews.

assailant One who makes a verbal or physical attack on another.

atomic bomb A bomb of enormous power. Its energy comes from a chemical reaction.

Axis The countries that fought on the side of Nazi Germany—for example, Japan and Italy.

bayonet A knife or sword that fits on the barrel of a rifle.

communist Having to do with or believing in communism, a social and economic system in which each person works and is paid according to his or her abilities and needs. There are no upper and lower classes, and all people share all property and resources. In most functioning communist nations, the country is run by a single-party government that makes all decisions for society.

concentration camp A place where political prisoners or others considered undesirable or enemies of the state are housed, usually under dreadful conditions.

crematorium An oven for burning dead bodies.

deportation Sending an individual, or a group of people, out of a country where they have no rights.

dictator A ruler who has absolute power, unlike a leader who can be defeated in an election.

extermination Mass murder or complete destruction.

freedom of speech The right to hold and state opinions without interference by the state, as recognized in international human rights law.

genocide The deliberate killing of a group of people, especially those of a particular ethnic group, religion, or belief system.

Gestapo Nazi secret state police.

ghetto An area in a city where people of similar social, political, or economic backgrounds live, usually in poor conditions.

humanitarian A person devoted to helping, relieving the suffering, and improving the lives of others.

Kristallnacht A pogrom against Jews in Germany and Austria in 1938.

The name translates as "night of the broken glass."

liberate To set free.

microfilm A film of documents at greatly reduced size.

Nazi Party Short for National Socialist German Workers Party.

non-aggression pact An agreement between nations not to go to war against each other.

oppression Unjust or cruel control of a person or group of people by those in power.

Palestine An area between the Mediterranean Sea and the Jordan River with historic and religious importance to Jews, Muslims, and Christians.

persecution Organized and systematic mistreatment of a person or group based on religious, ethnic or other background.

pogrom An official attack against a group, especially Jews.

prisoner of war A person who is held by the enemy during a war.

rampant Frequent, widely occurring.

resistance Organized groups working in secret to help the Allies fight the Nazis.

scorched earth A military strategy involving destruction of anything useful to the enemy after an army's retreat from an area.

socialism An economic system in which people share in the wealth of the community or country and the people, or workers, participate in decision-making; similar to communism but generally more flexible and open to multi-party democracies.

Soviet Union A former nation made up of a group of communist republics in parts of Europe and Asia. It was dissolved in 1991, creating a group of independent, non-communist nations out of its former republics, including Russia, Ukraine, Georgia, and Kazakhstan.

SS Short for *Schutzstaffel*, which means "protection squadron." Founded as a bodyguard service for Hitler, it grew into a brutal police force of 250,000 by the start of World War II in 1939.

synagogue A Jewish place of worship.

tuberculosis An infectious lung disease that can cause death if not treated.

typhus A sometimes fatal disease caused by a parasite carried by lice, common in unhygienic conditions.

uprising A revolt, usually against a government.

Zionist Relating to a political movement that supports a Jewish homeland.

Further Information

Books

Glowinski, Michal. *The Black Seasons* (Jewish Lives).
Evanston, IL: Northwestern University Press, 2005.

Mieszkowska, Anna. *Irena Sendler: Mother of the Children of the Holocaust*.
Westport, CT: Praeger, 2011.

Tomaszewski, Irene (editor and translator). *Inside a Gestapo Prison: The Letters of Krystyna Wituska, 1942–1944*. Detroit: Wayne State University Press, 2006.

Tomaszewski, Irene, and Tecia Werbowski. *Code Name: Zegota: Rescuing Jews in Occupied Poland, 1942–1945: The Most Dangerous Conspiracy in Wartime Europe*. Santa Barbara, CA: Praeger, 2010.

Videos

The Courageous Heart of Irena Sendler (DVD). Hallmark Hall of Fame, 2009.

Irena Sendler: In the Name of Their Mothers, a documentary film by Mary Skinner, featuring Irena Sendler (DVD). PBS, 2011.

Sendler's List (DVD). Michael Dudziewicz, 2002.

Websites

www.irenasendler.org
Run by the Lowell Milken Center, this website features the story behind Irena and the *Life in a Jar* Project as well as links to dates for performances of the *Life in a Jar* play, a photo gallery of moments in Irena's life and times, lists of books about children and the Holocaust, and other projects.

www.pbs.org/programs/irena-sendler/

The Public Broadcasting Service (PBS) website provides information, viewing times, and a link to purchase a DVD of their 2011 documentary entitled *Irena Sendler: In the Name of Their Mothers*. The film is based on the official authorized testimony of Irena Sendler and others who participated with her in the conspiracy to save children. It features the last interviews with Irena Sendler at the age of 95 in Warsaw.

www.irenasendlerfilm.com/

This is the home page for *Irena Sendler: In the Name of Their Mothers* from 2B Productions, the people who created the film. This site provides additional information concerning the subjects and the making of the film, short biographies of the filmmakers, updates as to future plans for the film, a trailer, and contact information.

www.yadvashem.org/

This is the home of Yad Vashem, Israel's official memorial to Jewish victims of the Holocaust. This site includes links to the Holocaust History Museum, online exhibits, videos, teaching materials, and the "Righteous among the Nations" Program—honored gentiles who helped save the lives of countless victims.

www.ushmm.org/

The United States Holocaust Memorial Museum site is an amazing resource for information about anything related to the Holocaust. It has a fantastic Learning Site for Students at *http://www.ushmm.org/outreach/en/*

www.sprawiedliwi.org.pl/en/cms/polish-righteous/

This site, called "The Polish Righteous," is linked to the website of the Museum of the History of Polish Jews in Warsaw, Poland. It is dedicated to enriching viewers' appreciation of non-Jewish Poles who saved Jewish lives during the Holocaust. It contains features about programs recognizing such people and stories about Irena Sendler and others honored with the title "Righteous among the Nations."

http://dornsife.usc.edu/vhi/

The USC Shoah Foundation Institute features powerful video clips of interviews with survivors of the Holocaust covering such topics as life before genocide, hiding, ghettos, camps, liberation, life after genocide, and loss.

Index

Index

About the Author

Susan Brophy Down lives on Vancouver Island in British
Columbia, Canada. As an award-winning newspaper and
magazine writer, she has covered a variety of topics such as
business, arts and culture and design.